Collecting
Lalique
Perfume Bottles & Glass

Robert Prescott-Walker

Francis Joseph
London
1-870703-14-6

© Francis Joseph Publications 2001

Second edition

Published in the UK by
Francis Joseph Publications
5 Southbrook Mews London SE12 8HG

Typeset by E J Folkard Computer Services
199 Station Road, Crayford, Kent DA1 3QF

Printed by Longo Group, Bolzano (Italy)

ISBN 1-870703-14-6

Acknowledgements

The one good thing about being able revise ones work is that things really can be brought up to date. What you will find in this edition are the recent market developments; additional chapters, such as 'Lalique and the Internet' and even more colour illustrations. You will also find plenty of added information throughout the text.

I am again indebted to Christie's and Bonhams for the use of their illustrations, with a special thanks to Mark Wilkinson for having allowed me to have some special request photographs. I am also very grateful to Nicholas M. Dawes for kindly allowing me to use some of his illustrations in this new edition.

Could I also thank Philippa J Hudson, the proof-reader of the original text.

As I mentioned previously, it is only possible to learn so much from books and other printed material, however I am hopeful that this edition will enable you to explore some avenues of interest that you may not have considered before. The only way to learn anything about objects is to get out and handle the goods. There is no greater way of learning about something, especially objects, than through touch and sight. Your tactile and visual senses will be able to develop a knowledge that can never be achieved through reading. For my money this is probably why buying and selling solely through Internet auctions and such like will never replace actually viewing an object before making the decision to buy. However, more of that later!

If there is one thing I hope to achieve through this book, it is that some of you will become more confident about picking up and learning from the objects you choose to collect, and as a consequence, take pleasure in learning and discovering more about the wares. Every object has its own story to tell, as long as the right questions are asked of it.

Robert Prescott-Walker

About the Author

Robert Prescott-Walker has studied the History of Visual Arts and Design at university, recently completing an MA in the History of Ceramics. Robert had formerly spent three years working in the Stoke-on-Trent City Museum and Art Gallery followed by eight years in the auction room world, an interest generated through summer jobs at Christie's, King Street, plus employment by Sotheby's and Bonham's where he specialised in the fields of Ceramics and Glass and the Decorative Arts.

Over the years Robert has developed various specific interests which have been formed from the basis of his study collection which includes: textiles, 1920-1970; tiles, plastics, furniture and a wide selection of ceramics and glass. He has been able to research and develop an in-depth knowledge of Art Pottery and Craft/Studio Pottery, from which he has gained a highly specialised knowledge of several early Art Potteries.

Robert is now a freelance antiques and decorative arts consultant, offering a wide variety of client services through various means, either as a lecturer for specialist societies or more general talks to clubs and charitable groups. Having a widely recognised knowledge within his field he has developed a steady stream of private enquiries regarding the identification and valuation of a wide variety of items.

Until moving to New York with his wife Christina, vice president, Head of European Ceramics and Chinese Export Porcelain, Sotheby's, Robert had been lecturing at Loughborough University College of Art and Design in ceramic history and design history.

Contents

Lalique glass must surely be among the most complete and affordable of works of art available today. Using mass-production methods to full potential, together with the application of highly innovative artistic designs, today we can look back on this extraordinary, indeed revolutionary, contribution to the history of glass manufacture. All the result of one man's achievements, René Lalique.

Introduction

René Lalique was a master craftsman, a great innovator and a vigorous entrepreneur of twentieth-century commercial glass. His legacy is still very much alive and with us today, both in the volume and variety of his work that can still be found and in the current production of Lalique glass.

The secret of his success and international reputation lies in his ability to combine artistic flair with mass-production methods of manufacture. His individual style, together with an acute knowledge of the advantages and limitations of the various methods of production he employed have left us with a wide variety of shapes and an enormous range of designs, in a variety of surface textures and colours. The breadth and diversity of his work, from the high-volume popular items through to the limited one-off designs, makes his wares widely sought after by collectors.

What I am going to be looking at in this book is a sample of Lalique's commercial glass, as opposed to the rare *cire perdue* glass and early individual jewellery works of art: the type of item you are most likely to come across out there in the market or, the sort of object you might hope to spot on a dim early morning at the setting up of your favourite antique fair or in the dark confines of your local bric-à-brac shop after a recent house clearance. Not every piece has a clear signature. It may have been concealed beneath the constant grinding of being moved to and fro on a mantelpiece, for instance, and in such circumstances it may go undetected.

What I hope to be able to do is to instil in those who want to learn the ability to look at a piece of Lalique glass, make an educated judgement about it and be confident enough either to buy it or put it down and wait for another day. Too often we pick up an object only to timidly put it down (although we really would like to own it), with the words, "I don't know really. I like it, but I'm not sure". In other words we don't think we have the necessary skills to properly assess the object. Now is your chance to acquire new skills or, to be more precise, learn how to use skills you already have. The ultimate aim being to gain confidence in our newly tuned skills and therefore start to enjoy handling objects.

Collecting should above all be enjoyable and exciting. I hope I can dispel some of the anxiety and worry that most tentative potential buyers have when they approach a new and sometimes expensive field of collecting. But I can only impart facts about what to look for and how to look based on my own experiences and mistakes. Never be afraid of making mistakes; they are best viewed as a positive experience from which you can learn and move on. Hopefully, having read this you won't make any! The major part of the homework has to be done by you. All you need is an inquisitive attitude together with lots and lots of practice, that is handling and asking about as many pieces as you can.

Only by picking up and handling the objects can you ever hope to learn anything about the objects. Handling an object is the best memory aid you will ever have. Your visual memory, whether you realise it or not, is your greatest asset. Feeling the weight and balance, the texture of the surface, the crispness or smoothness of the modelling, judging the depth of colour, etc., are some of the essentials that you need to become familiar with in order to gain confidence in what you are looking at and handling.

What to look out for, both in terms of the condition and in the aesthetics of the piece, will only take a surprisingly short time to develop, as long as you take your homework seriously. Use the above criteria to judge the merits of a piece and what it is worth to you, how far you should bid or what the right price for you would be. By condition I mean both the result of its manufacture, i.e. faults, blemishes or even a certain intended effect that you don't want on your pieces, and also the effects of the passage of time on the object, the wear and tear of daily use. Where do such blemishes most frequently appear, and how do you find them? For many objects this may be fairly obvious: after all if you design something like a car mascot that is going to sit on top of the radiator of some Bugatti, Bentley or Talbot, tearing around stony country lanes, you would expect the odd chip from a piece of gravel. Just as you would expect the inner neck of a scent bottle, being used every day to have gained a few nicks over the years.

I have been handling Lalique glass for over ten years, a mere drop in the ocean when compared to many avid collectors of his ware. But whether you are a recent collector wanting to know a little more about the topic or a collector of some experience, I hope you will be able to benefit from the information in this book. After all, the most astute collector, in whatever field, will always have their eyes open in the hope of learning or seeing something new, gaining another small step on the pyramid of knowledge and another advantage point over the competition.

All that is left for me to say is, once armed with the hints in this book, pick up every piece of Lalique glass you can get your hands on and have a good look. If you have picked up a similar object before, compare it to the first one and see if you can spot some differences. You don't need to make any special effort to memorise or note down the features you find of interest – having picked up and handled the piece, your visual memory will do the rest.

Chronology

1860   René Jules Lalique was born at Ay on 6th April in the Champagne region of France.

1862   The Lalique family moved to the suburbs of Paris, where René went to school at the Lycée Turgot near Vincennes.

1876   The death of his father. René apprenticed to the jeweller and goldsmith Louis Aucoc. René also enrolled at the Ecole des Arts Décoratifs.

1880   Left Paris for Sydenham School of Art, London, formerly the Crystal Palace School of Art. The school closed and René returned to Paris as a freelance designer, also enrolling at the Ecole Bernard Palissy, where he studied sculpture and modelling.

1881   Designed for some of the leading jewellery houses such as: Aucoc, Boucheron, Cartier, Jules Destape and Hamelin.

1885   Purchased the workshop of Jules Destape on the Place Gaillon, Destape retiring to Algeria.

1887   Exhibited his new jewellery at the Exposition Nationale des Arts Industriels in Paris. Opened another workshop on the Rue du Quatre Septembre.

1890   Both the above premises would appear to have closed in favour of new ones at 20 Rue Terese, Paris, where he began serious experiments with the cire perdue (lost wax) technique. Married the daughter of sculptor Auguste Ledru.

1894   Exhibited at the Salon de la Société des Artistes Français.

1896   Exhibited again at the Salon.

1897   Won the highly prestigious award of the Croix de Chevalier de la Légion d'Honneur.

1900   Exhibited at the Exposition Universelle, Paris.

1902   Continued his experiments with the cire perdue technique in the village of Clairfontaine, just south of Paris. Developed architectural glass, made until 1912. Opened exhibition outlet at 40 Cours la Reine, also the Lalique family home from 1902 until his death in 1945.

1905   Lalique opened his first Paris retail outlet at 24 Place Vendôme.

1907   Design of scent bottles for François Coty.

1909   Rented a glassworks at Combs-la-Ville, east of Paris.

1910   Started to manufacture a wide range of perfume bottles and powder boxes. It would also appear that this was where he started to make cire perdue vessels for the first time.

1912   Lalique started to manufacture glass in the 'modern style'. Exhibited at the Pavilion de Marsan. First exhibition of glass at the Place Vendôme saw the emergence of the Lalique 'style'.

1915   The factory at Combs-la-Ville was forced to close with the outbreak of war.

1919   Coms-la-Ville re-opened. In the same year building work began on a new factory at Wingen-sur-Moder in the Alsace region of France.

1921   Work began at the new factory, where it continues to this day.

1922   René Lalique's son Marc joins the business.

1923   A retrospective exhibition of his work was held at the Pavillion de Marsan in the Musée des Arts Décoratifs in Paris.

1925   The Exposition des Arts Décoratifs et Industriels, Paris. The most important exhibition of Lalique glass, with his designs appearing in many of the pavilions and external structures, often on a massive scale, establishing his international reputation.

1937   The closure of the Combs-la-Ville glassworks, due to reduced demand.

1940   The closure of the Wingen factory with the outbreak of the Second World War.

1945   René Lalique died on 9th May, aged 85, only days after the surrender of Germany to the Allies. René's son Marc, formerly the plant manager and administrator, took over the company and by the late 1940s had rebuilt the Wingen factory. He also radically changed the glass mixture adding twice the lead oxide content, making it Cristal glass.

1951   The new look of the Lalique company was revealed in the Art of Glass exhibition at the Pavilion de Marsan.

1956   Marc's daughter Marie-Claude joined the factory and soon began designing with her father.

1977   Marie-Claude took control of the factory on the death of her father.

Setting the Stage

If we are to learn anything about the work of René Lalique it is important to know something of the foundations that made it possible for him to begin building and developing his own characteristic style. Only through a true understanding and appreciation of the works and influences that formed the basis of his art will the true importance of his work be revealed.

Just what had been going on before René Lalique started on his quest to make his individual stylistic design statements? After all, all innovative and seemingly original ideas and works of art have in the main developed from influences of the past. This can be divided into two very different, but equally important, approaches to the making of glass, namely the continuation of traditional glass manufacture through to high-volume production of uniformly repeated moulded glass together with a totally new approach to the glass body itself, along with its function, purpose, technique and use of colour, inclusions, decorative surface techniques and decorative effect.

The making of objects in glass prior to the mid-nineteenth century revolved around the skill and training of individual glass-makers. Those individual skills, with each country developing a characteristic national style, were passed on through long apprenticeships, every generation developing new skills tuned by changes in demand and fashion. New shapes were born out of chance and/or direct experimentation during the act of making, as was much of the internal and external decorative effects.

By the beginning of the nineteenth century, communication and travel having become more accessible to all, the skilled craftsmen began to cross the borders of new countries, searching for profitable opportunities to make the most of their talents. Towards the mid-nineteenth century, with the rapid exchange of new techniques and styles of decoration available throughout Europe, not only in glass but various other media, there was a veritable cacophony of revivalist styles mixed with nationalistic fashions, but all with little artistic direction. Glass technology advanced rapidly as a result of constant research, resulting in new and diverse decorative effects. Glass was cut or engraved, crystal, coloured, flashed, enamelled, acid-etched and stained in a seemingly endless diversity. Demand for symmetry and classical proportion of shape, embellished with exquisite and often complex engraved patterns or scenes, developed into the flamboyant geometric deep-cut glass vessels, so popular by the time of the Great Exhibition of 1851, forming the foundation of the heavy cut glass that is still favoured today. The public appetite for consistency of form and standardisation of pattern coincided with the introduction of machine-made glass. The introduction of volume production, mechanically made and standardised glass opened a new era in the manufacture of glass, but was only exploited to its full extent and artistic potential in the work of René Lalique.

At the same time the new machine mass-production methods brought about an opposing movement, whose aim was to reassess the true use and artistic potential of the glass material. Artists and writers, both in France and Britain, wanted to stimulate original and creative artistic work influenced by the study of nature. This new concept, which was bitterly opposed to the products of pre-industrial revivalism and the lifeless repetitive mechanical glass, was given direction by the newly re-opened trade with Japan and China.

The influence of Japanese and Chinese works of art was to have an important and lasting effect, not only stimulating a new approach to form and decoration in glass, painting and almost every field of decorative arts but in irrevocably transforming the spiritual understanding and attitudes Western artists and designers had for their art. In glass this involved a shift away from mainstream commercial products, with the establishment of a separate tributary embracing two new art forms: Art or Studio glass and mechanical commercial glass. There was however one man whose work was to straddle both, René Lalique.

One of the earliest recognised protagonists of this new, more expressive and experimental approach to glass was Joseph Brocard. Brocard, having revived the art of enamelling on glass, initially turning out imitations of early Syrian ware, exhibited in Paris in 1867 at the World Exhibition, later producing more individual and original works. Only five years prior to this the widespread influence of Japanese art, now established in the West for some ten years, was evident in the public sensation caused by the display of Japanese works at the London International exhibition of 1862. This led to the publication of a wide variety of books concerning the art of Japan, later to be termed 'Japonism'.

In France an organisation for the improvement of design was established in 1863. To be called the Union Centrale des Arts Décoratifs, it led to the founding of libraries and museums, the publication of a magazine and most importantly established a regular exhibition programme of contemporary work. The new lease of life brought about an explosion of experimentation and rejuvenation of style, the results of which were new and exciting, genuinely creative and personally expressive styles in glass. The tradition and function of shape was transformed, techniques of surface decoration and the use of colour became complex and subtle in the new freedom of self-expression. Symmetry and geometry were metamorphosed into irregular amorphous forms, function taking a back seat. The clean transparent quality of traditional brilliant cut and engraved glass was cast aside in favour of coloured and/or opaque glass, often employing several colours with soft tonal changes as well as multiple layering of coloured glass. The surface was applied with low- and high-relief coloured glass, carved, acid-etched, engraved, enamelled and gilded, with some glass artists employing several of these techniques on one piece.

The greatest exponents of these new highly sophisticated and complicated studies in glass were Emile Gallé and François-Eugène Rousseau. In the 1878 Union Centrale exhibition they received the first serious critical appreciation of their work. This early work was fresh and exuberant: although freely borrowing from previous sources the styles were used as inspiration but never slavishly copied. Gallé's love of poetry, often derived from the writings of the Symbolists which formed the basis of his own philosophy and ideals, frequently inspired certain pieces, the poem being incorporated into the design. But his love of nature, combined with the introduction of new soft colours, led to some of his most lyrical and inspirational work. It is through the work of Gallé and Rousseau that we can see the initial development of the foundations of the modern concept of Art glass.

This new challenge of artistic freedom of expression was taken up and explored still further by artists such as Henri Gros, who introduced a new process of firing powdered glass in a mould called *pâte de verre*, subsequently to be used by Albert Dammouse, François Décorchemont and Alméric Walter. Gallé's work itself was copied by various glass-makers in Sweden, Belgium and Norway, the closest of which was the work of Jean Daum, in neighbouring Nancy. E. Leveille carried on the work of Rousseau to much popular acclaim, many pieces of his work being acquired by several museums at the Paris Exhibition of 1900. Maurice Marinot, a contemporary of Lalique and an equal giant in his own field, continued the exploration of individual self-expression in glass through the use of light, colour, texture and lyrical form, initiated by the work of Rousseau. Marinot's work can be seen as the precursor of present Studio glass, its roots in Italian, Swedish, Finnish and British glass of the 1950s and 1960s.

Not to be outdone, the commercial manufacturers had also been developing their own innovative methods of production: in particular, blown and press-moulded glass, formerly used in ancient times, but in the production of hollow wares first used in about 1820 in America. Initially moulded glass was used to manufacture cheap bottles, medical wares and containers in large numbers and at a rapid rate. Perhaps more importantly this technique brought about the introduction of wares made by unskilled labour. In 1864, when the first patent was issued in America for a steam-operated press, glass became affordable to all, but caused unrest in the industry, workmen fearing for their jobs. The wares produced showed little awareness of possibilities of the process, merely being used to make disposable items and imitations of expensive glass.

The glass scent bottles produced by René Lalique in association with François Coty in 1907, seen against the background of what was currently being made by mechanical press-moulding, provide evidence of the huge technical achievements and significant technological understanding that Lalique had of the process. The importance of Lalique's achievements can be seen by his re-discovery of *demi-crystal*, which meant that delicate and repetitive designs could be manufactured on a huge scale. This material had 30 per cent less lead oxide, leaving a highly ductile material which needed little attention after release from the mould. The way was now open for a visionary craftsman to combine the potential techniques of mass-produced commercial glass with a mastery of artistic ability.

The aim of the exponents of this new artistic pursuit in glass was to create individual pieces that expressed the conscious artistry and thoughts of their creators, revealing the medium at its most flamboyant and grandiose. However, this highly individual art did not transpose itself for commercial mass production. Gallé's attempts at commercial production of single, double and triple overlay watery landscapes, flowers and berries pieces are in themselves huge achievements, but in only a remote visual sense do they reflect the spirit of Japanese art.

What René Lalique accomplished had not been achieved or even attempted before, and to this day rarely occurs. Lalique through his own purpose of mind and intent built a bridge over the chasm dividing Art and Industry. The one ever in the service of providing a one-off exclusive item, born of handicraft and a single mind; the other a process engaged in repetitive production at minimal cost and in large quantities, offering items at affordable prices to a broad spectrum of consumers, but still with the characteristic style of Lalique. Whilst he could be, and indeed for a time was, solely involved in the making of one-off artistic pieces, both in jewellery and glass, his true intention was to make his art universal by making available to a wide spectrum of the general public every conceivable decorative and functional glass object associated with the interior decoration of a house or indeed part of the structure. On occasion, especially with his prestigious exhibition works and private commissions, this inspired Lalique to see just how far he could stretch the boundaries of his production Art-glass techniques.

Through the work that René Lalique has left for us to judge today, and armed with a knowledge of the foundations on which he set his artistic standards, we can start to appreciate the significance of what he achieved throughout his life and how it came about. Leaving in his legacy to us a huge diversity of designs, seen in both a high volume of mass-produced items or individually crafted and sculpted work.

Lalique – An Overview

René Jules Lalique was born on 6th April, 1860, in the rural setting of Ay in the Champagne region of France, from where his mother originated. In 1862 the Lalique family moved to the suburbs of Paris, where René went to school at the Lycée Turgot near Vincennes. René showed early promise at school with his studies of nature, including flowers, insects and animals, winning a design award by the age of 12. Misfortune was to hit the family with the early death of his father in 1876, which forced René, no doubt at the insistence of his mother, to seek an apprenticeship with the fashionable jeweller and goldsmith Louis Aucoc. At the same time René also enrolled at the Ecole des Arts Décoratifs.

Two years later René left Paris for Sydenham on the outskirts of London, where there was a strong French community. Little is known of this period, but it would appear that he carried on his studies at the School of Art in Sydenham. The college closed in 1880, with René returned to Paris. Whilst in London, René would undoubtedly have been very aware of the work of the followers of William Morris, the Pre-Raphaelites and, more importantly, the Symbolist movement and the influence of Japanese art. French Impressionist artists were also making frequent visits to England at this time, such was the cross-fertilisation of ideas and influences. Out of this René was to form the basis of his own personal blend of stylised Art Nouveau and Japonism, together with the skills and ideals of the Arts and Crafts Movement, which advocated the study of nature in all forms, a concept already nurtured by René.

René returned to France in 1880 in order to become a freelance designer. He initially found work designing wallpaper and fabrics for M. Vuilleret, at the same time enrolling at the Ecole Bernard Palissy to study sculpture and modelling techniques. Before long René had created designs for his former employer Louis Aucoc and other leading jewellers, such as Cartier, Boucheron, Destape and Hamelin. In 1885, with the purchase of Jules Destape's workshop, on the Place Gaillon, René embarked on his first serious experiments using semi-precious materials combined with what was to become the Lalique style. Having advertised his work in the trade journal Le Bijou and exhibited at venues such as the Exhibition Nationale des Arts Industriels in 1887, René soon gained a reputation and clients for his work. So much so that he opened another workshop on the Rue de Quatre Septembre, to be followed by the closure of both premises in favour of a single one at 20 Rue Terese, Paris, with enough room for 30 workmen.

His clients now included the great actress Sarah Bernhardt, for whom he was to design many stunning and original pieces, the Armenian multi-millionaire,

Calouste Gulbenkian, the Rothschilds and Queen Alexandra. His work during the period covering the turn of the century seemed to flit from one influence to another, with no particular linking theme or direction. The works during this period can either be seen as one-off artistic creations or the experimental thoughts of an artist still yet to find his true purpose.

So popular had his work become, winning various awards such as the Légion d'honneur in 1897, that his work was now highly sought after and exhibited in major galleries. To hold an exhibition of his work, even at this early stage in his career, was the height of fashion, and heralded as much for his reputation as his designs. And this was only the first part of a two-part career. Undaunted by his elevated status, René continued to be more and more interested in the use of glass in its own right, unfettered from its metal mounts and fixtures in multi-media settings. He revived the art of cire perdue or 'lost wax', initially used in conjunction with his jewellery designs and later for objects and sculptures in their own right. The popularity of his jewellery led to many cheap imitators, which, whilst flattering, seemed to hasten a change in direction for René.

In 1902 he continued his experiments with the cire perdue technique, with much success, at a small workshop in the village of Clairfontaine, just south of Paris. Here he also began to develop architectural glass, producing unique frosted cast panels with pine branches in low relief for his own studio and retail outlet at 40 Cours la Reine. This five-storey building was to be René's home from 1902 until his death in 1945. It was also here, from 1907, that he was to become involved with the design of scent bottles for François Coty and thereby take on the demands of volume production required by industry. To design for industry requires a completely different set of criteria to that of small-scale studio work.

In order for René to become a fully fledged verrier there was one last step he had to take, the move to larger premises and the use of machine technology for mass production. This he did in 1909, renting a glassworks at Combs-la-Ville, east of Paris. In the following year, having started to manufacture a wide range of perfume bottles and powder boxes, he was able to purchase the glassworks and later to expand it. Only six years after the factory opened it was forced to close with the outbreak of war.

The years leading up to 1902 can be seen as the formative studio craftsman's apprenticeship, the fertile, creative ground of the individual artist, expressing through complex and simple use of both techniques and materials the highly personal characteristic style of the artist, ever seeking the best mode of expression for his designs. This René found through the unlikely combination of his art with the mass-production techniques of industry.

The perfumer René Coty commissioned Lalique to re-design the graphics used to promote and label his products. As a result of this project, undertaken in 1907, Lalique came to re-design the bottles as well. Lalique's studio was not equipped to make blown wares on a commercial scale and these first examples of his industrial design were made by the Parisian glassworks of Legras & Co. In 1909 Lalique purchased the Verrerie de Combs-la-Ville, and he was soon approached by other perfumers – Forvil, d'Orsay, Vijny, etc. By 1912 he had ceased making jewellery and other artefacts and thereafter concentrated his efforts on the design and manufacture of glass. Lalique, unlike other designers of glass and equipped with his knowledge of the lost wax techniques and materials used to produce detailed jewellery, was to become a figure of great importance in the next stage of his career following the closure of his glassworks in 1914.

Following the Armistice, Lalique purchased a full-size industrial plant at Wingen-sur-Moder in the traditional glass-making region of Alsace. Despite the upheaval of the war, the factory was a going concern and he was able to assemble a workforce experienced in several aspects of manufacture. From the start, his intentions were to produce fine quality glass at a price the majority could afford. Wherever possible he used the mass-production techniques of pressing, centrifuge casting and mould blowing, but only if they could be employed without loss of standards in design or quality of production.

Lalique pioneered work in casting and developed the technique of spinning molten glass into the mould (centrifuge casting). This technique was used to make large light shades and bowls with deep relief decoration of the sort used in the foyers of commercial and public buildings and the salons of ocean liners. Most of his small-scale ornamental glass was made by a mixture of the usual pressing and mould-blowing techniques, but to a much higher standard of finish than was common with pressed glass of the period. Lalique was always careful to produce designs that made use of the advantages of production techniques, without forcing them beyond the limits of what was possible.

The range of products made at Lalique's glassworks was greater than any other manufacturer could boast. He made car mascots, dressing-table sets, tableware, lamp shades, ornamental sculpture, and a variety of household ornaments. The designs reflect the mood of the time and the decade in which they originated.

René Lalique's unique achievement, and the reason for his success, was to bring together the two parallel developments of artistic glass and mass-production techniques, which together produced an item that was both artistic and affordable. Mass-production methods had their limitations, but Lalique was ever conscious of this, deciding which shapes could be made by which method. He even went one step further, utilising advantages in one method of production to accentuate certain designs, whilst restricting other designs within the limitations of the machine. Through careful choice and an informed understanding of the techniques, he managed to produce pieces which combined designs of great originality and balance with pleasing lines and tonal variations of colour, on a wide variety of innovative shapes. The subtlety and ethereal quality achieved in many of his pieces is all the more remarkable when you pick up a piece and realise just how heavy they are. Many of his machine-made pieces are really quite heavy, certainly heavier than the initial impression you feel when studying the design and effect created by the frosted grounds or subtlety of the colours.

Whilst many other books on Lalique praise his magnificent achievements in jewellery design, his huge and impressive exhibition water fountains or complete interior designs, these are but the tangible results. It is the thoughts and ideas that were the birth of a historic development that was to prove of great importance in the world of glass, namely the fundamental ideals and achievement of applying artistic designs to commercial manufactured glass.

The Legacy of Lalique

Surely the most telling indicator of the quality of Lalique's glass is the extent to which his work can still be found in countries all over the world and in many settings, from the ordinary home to the local museum.

Whether reflecting stylistic contemporary trends or a more individual character, René Lalique's designs have a classic timeless quality that is unaffected by ever changing fashions. The forms he used are both simple and well proportioned, the function and utility of the piece being his main consideration.

Lalique was able, through a complete understanding of technique and his strong personality, to reveal the beauty of the glass in its own right. His careful use of design, taking full account of the sheer solidity and crystalline purity of the glass, resulted in a vast range of lavish, rich and delicately crafted works that were conceived for mass production, to be available to all.

Whilst the style of design was characteristically his, it is also emphatically French. His glass derived from a combination of the new awareness and freedom of expression seen in the work of Gallé, Rousseau and others, exploring the potential of the glass medium and the technical limitations and restrictions imposed on glass in the new machine methods of manufacturing.

Just as this combination of artistry, self-expression and new experimental techniques created the foundation of modern Art glass, so the work of Lalique had a significant influence on twentieth-century commercially designed glass.

The traditional glass that we associate with René Lalique is still very much alive in the current production of the Wingen glassworks, now designed by René's granddaughter, Marie-Claude, in her own highly personal style.

Collectors and Collecting

The glass we now collect and treat with such reverence, our prized pieces cushioned on felt-covered shelves, placed in lockable display cabinets, with the interior lights adjusted to maximise the effect, most of these pieces were bought and sold as everyday functional objects, fruit to be placed in bowls, candles burning in candle-holders, scent gently puffed from bottles and aromatically sprayed from atomisers. They were objects that were dusted, washed-up, rinsed, dried and placed back on the shelf ready for the new flowers.

More often than not the original prices paid for many objects as well as their design or colour indicated that they were meant to be treated with the utmost care, but after a sufficient period of time having been dusted and cleaned by a change of hands or two, and with changing fashions making way for the new and latest popular design and colours, their initial importance was often overlooked. This is how, for example, much of the original hand-staining has long since disappeared or been left with the merest hint of what it might once have been like. Chips, bruising, cracking, etc., indicate authentic wear and tear, making perfect examples rarer and as such, commanding a premium.

For all those collectors who have had much pleasure in building up a fine and cherished collection of perfect pieces, there are equally as many collectors who like to use their pieces for their original purpose: flowers in a vase, gentle clouds of smoke wafting above the incense/ perfume burner, or the clock ticking on the mantelpiece, with letters and photographs wedged in behind. For such collectors, pleasure is derived from seeing how the objects were originally intended to be used, rather than in any ultimate monetary value. For the former collector it is both the pleasure derived from owning and examining such pieces for their artistic qualities and, if all is well, the value and future return that will be achieved in years to come from like-minded collectors, once the objects are returned to the market. In some sense there is certainly an investing element in connection with this type of glass, as *cire perdue* or rare production pieces inevitably command some of the highest values.

Many collectors will start to buy various pieces initially, before deciding on their own personal choice, often due to moderate prices. The first thing to decide when starting a collection is where and how it is going to be housed/displayed. Glass has its own particular qualities that need to be thought about: weight is certainly a consideration, as is its translucency. It is no good placing heavy glass vases on a dimly lit shelf above a window, on the landing or in a glazed, unlit cabinet.

Do you want to collect certain stylistic designs, floral subjects, animal subjects or abstract designs? How do you display car mascots, especially those that have a tendency to fall over? How available are the pieces you decide to collect likely to be? What type of condition are you going to find acceptable? These are just some of the questions that are worth considering before you set out on the exciting and rewarding road of collecting Lalique glass.

Scent Bottles

The significance of René Lalique to the perfume bottle industry is that it was he, along with Mr. Coty, who revolutionised the industry. Between them they transformed the way perfume was sold, made and marketed; developing it into the highly commercial, high profile, designer-marketed product that it is today. Until the start of this partnership (in about 1907/08 when Lalique had his outlet at 24 Place Vendôme, Paris), perfume was sold to the buyer by filling the client's own perfume flask with the perfume of their choice from a large bottle in one of the few perfumeries in the nearest large town or city. The advent of the specifically designed bottle, in this case using glass, for an individual manufacturer and a particular perfume, which also might have its own designed packaging, meant that the manufacturer could specifically market and sell the packaged items in far more and far smaller outlets in small towns and villages. The buyer did not need to carry their empty flask long distances to be refilled. Instead, the buyer now was able to choose from a selection of perfumes; one for every occasion, mood and season should they so desire. The bottles themselves became an important selling and marketing feature, to some extent taking over in importance from the contents. By vastly increasing the numbers of perfumes available together with mastering the art of making new synthetic fragrances, the manufacturer could also sell the perfumes at a much reduced cost. The first manufacturer to achieve this was François Coty.

The story of Lalique and the manufacture of scent bottles can be divided into two parts, with the labeling being an important and integral part of the bottle. In the first place Lalique made specific bottles to order for manufacturers. Initially for Coty, only a few years later Lalique was designing bottles for over a dozen of the worlds leading perfume manufacturers, including names such as Roger et Gallet, D'Orsay and Worth. Added to this were the numerous stores that ordered their own bottles and perfume either for exclusive sale or for special promotional events. Two of these were Jay Thorpe and Saks, both in New York.

The other part of the story, as far as collecting is concerned, relates to the bottles Lalique designed and made to be sold, empty, through all his own outlets. These bottles make up by far the greater number of perfume bottles. Just to put things into perspective for the moment, Lalique is known to have designed perfume bottles for over 60 companies and produced at least 360 different bottles in total with the research still on-going.

Some of the most sought after bottles are those designed by Lalique for sale in his own outlets. This is due to the fewer numbers that are likely to have been made compared to some of those manufactured for one of the commercial perfume firms. Another issue relates to the length of time some of the bottles made for the perfume firms were in production. Those which were available for twenty or thirty years are much easier to find today.

In recent years there has been a growing trend for many collectors to collect the '"Total Image", as so aptly expressed by Mary Lou and Glenn Utt in the preface to the sale of their collection of Lalique perfume bottles held at Sotheby's New York, December 1998. The "Total Image" essentially means everything that one would have bought when buying a scent bottle from a retailer and in as pristine and unused a condition as possible, including if available the original bill of sale. Added to this is be the aim to collect as much related promotional and advertising material as possible. The reasoning behind this is that, thanks to René Lalique and Mr. Coty, the marketing, packaging and promotion of perfume was totally transformed from the humble pharmaceutical-based plain bottle into a vibrant and powerful industry, spawning a wealth of companies and the huge commercial industry that still exists today.

Some of the packaging of the bottles is really quite remarkable and an art in itself. The packaging should to be studied for its overall inventiveness of shape, the elaborateness of its method of opening; and its presentation: not to mention the graphics and use of colour, in co-ordination with the colour of the contents and /or bottle. After taking all this into account, only then can the art and collectablity of the perfume bottle be appreciated. Marketing such bottles was highly important. The ability to capture the right mood and style of the time, through the design of the bottle and its packaging and promotion, became a highly skilled business.

When the collecting of scent bottles really began in the late 1970s, there was, as remains, an element of affordability in terms of being able to collect a large number of items, which together with the small size of the bottles and ease of display, can be said to have made this field particularly straight forward to collect. The auction houses were not slow to spot this growing trend with Bonhams developing 'Commercial Scent Bottle' sales in the early 1990s. It had been noticed that in specialist Lalique sales during the 1980s, the scent bottle section always yielded some very high prices, due to the growing numbers of general scent bottle collectors. Therefore, the idea of combining into one sale all the manufacturers of scent bottles, together with the accompanying packaging and promotional material, was deemed to be of sufficient interest to warrant a sale. It was in these sales, which only lasted three years, that the concept of the 'Total Image' could be best seen.

As with other areas of Lalique glass, there are plenty of pitfalls for the unwary. The worst of the problems that might be encountered are wrongly marked bottles. In other words bottles made by another manufacturer to which someone has later added an imitation Lalique mark. One of the only ways of avoiding such bottles is to become very familiar with all the known illustrated Lalique bottles. Another way would be to become familiar with the various Lalique marks to a point where a spurious mark could be confidently identifed. The latter might take more time than the former. After this, the next main hurdle will be the all important condition, or rather the ability to recognise when something is not as it should be. In terms of scent bottles, some of the worst things that can happen are the significant alteration of the shape of the body, the neck and/or the stopper, due to the action of grinding. Illustrated in this book are a good and a bad version of 'Trois Guêpes', i.e. one with the wings of the wasps and one without. Very subtle differences that can make a vast difference in price! The illustration of the 'Cyclamen' bottle where virtually the whole neck has been ground away is another subtle and costly alteration.

At the same time care must be taken not to be too condemning as there are several bottles that were designed with two different stoppers, usually also in different colours, but not always. Examples of these being 'Four Figures', produced in black and clear glass, with large elaborate flat stoppers, and 'Eucalyptus' made for D'Oray, 'Bouchon Trois Hirondelles' as well as 'Bouchon Fleurs de Pommier' have to be watched as their outer edges can be very skillfully reduced to take out value depreciating chips.

Many of the other problems that are encountered are general and a note has been made of these in the 'Buying at auction' chapter. Some of the other problems relate not to the glass but to the packaging. Silk tassels often get replaced with modern examples, boxes can be completely wrong or have the wrong box for the perfume. Perfume bottle seals might have been altered, made-up or moved from one bottle to another. The applied gilt labels often found fixed on the front of a bottle can be moved from one bottle to another or be used as seals. Atomisers have their own inherent problems, mostly damage to the glass where the metal fixes over the neck, but also the replacement of the rubber puffer which will usually have perished, if there is one at all. The only way you are going to be sure everything is as perfect as it can be is to become very familiar with how all the above 'should' look. It really is a matter of education through the handling and study of as many scent bottles and related ware as possible.

The pricing of perfume bottles is dependent on a number of factors that will alter the price tag. Condition is a major factor in terms of depreciation, whilst consistency of colour and/or opacity, variation of colour and/or staining are all factors, some quite personal, that will alter the end price. In general bottles produced for high mass-production will be more common and therefore more easily found and accurately priced.

Collecting perfume bottles can give some of the most pleasing results of all the Lalique products if only because of the variety of interesting ways such a collection can be developed. Those made for a specific perfume company; those remaining as they were when they were sold complete with contents and printed material or those of specific forms. Whatever the final collection, the arrangement and display needs to be considered, as the final display, lighting and setting can be equally as important as the artifacts themselves.

How to Become a Lalique Expert

Whether confronted by a single item of Lalique or a large group, your reaction should be to learn as much as you can from the objects. Even if they are not the sort you intend to collect, there is always a great deal that can be learnt that might help in gaining a better understanding and appreciation of the pieces you are particularly interested in.

Equally it is very important to look at pieces that have been made by other manufacturers influenced by the Lalique style, as well as by those who made copies of Lalique's work. While copies can be interpreted as the greatest form of flattery, for Lalique such pieces were annoying, only spurring him on to produce yet more and better designs. To be confident about what you are handling it is as well to familiarise yourself with the variations in weight, surface texture, colour and brilliance of the glass, along with the quality of moulding and detail. Many of the pieces were honest copies, and clearly marked as such, produced to satisfy public demand. Unfortunately there were also direct copies made, usually left unmarked, many of which in the last twenty or thirty years have some spurious marks, added to deceive the unprepared. To appreciate the competition and imitators you will learn more about the real McCoy.

To add to the confusion there are also a number of pieces designed and made by René Lalique that were also produced after the Second World War. These later pieces, made using the Marc Lalique 'crystal', are harder and brighter in appearance and lack the moulded detail, the imitation frosted look betraying a more shiny satin aspect. Even today a few early designs, such as 'Nemours' or 'Bacchantes', are still being made. Therefore a visit to the Lalique gallery in Bond Street, London, or in New York will give you the opportunity of familiarising yourself with these pieces.

This section of the guide is designed to help you appreciate some of the things that you will find when you start to look at Lalique glass more closely. This includes technical features to look out for, factory flaws, types of damage and later alterations, all of which affect the condition and pricing of a piece. When talking about condition and quality it is worth pointing out that there are various criteria that when assessed should go to fixing a realistic market price. If several pieces of the same design are placed side by side the differences can be only too apparent.

The biggest area of contention when talking about condition is where and when polishing, thereby altering the appearance or size of piece, may have occurred. Many of the fluctuations are due to the process of manufacture and subsequent finishing. The technique of finishing or polishing a piece at the factory was a highly skilled hand process which was achieved by judgement of eye and hand, with some pieces needing more treatment than others. Generally speaking most pieces needed very little attention, due to the nature of the 'demi-crystal' and the use of metal moulds, where any sharp edges were removed by chamfering the edge.

Later polishing as a consequence of minor damage, whilst it means that the piece is probably not in the same state as when it left the factory, is often generally acceptable to many collectors. When pieces have had chunks or a large part removed, features altered or size reduced then the piece should always be labelled with the alterations that have taken place and priced accordingly. Inevitably it is always up to the buyer to make sure they are aware of such alterations.

What is acceptable in the extent and degree of alteration is entirely up to the buyer. The trick is in being able to satisfy yourself concerning the condition and quality, so that you can arrive at what you think an accurate price should be. Some collectors are extremely particular about the condition of a piece, making sure that it is in as much of a mint, untouched and pristine state as posssible, with just the right strength of colour and tint. There are just as many collectors, if not many more, who accept the slight wear and tear of the passing years, and many who don't mind the odd crack and chip or two. Whichever group you fit into, it is as well to know what to look for and how to find out about the condition, so that you can be totally confident about your assessment of a piece and satisfy yourself about the correct pricing level.

What to look for

The most common sign of wear on a piece of glass is surface scratching, usually visible in the base of the foot and sometimes on the side of objects and interior of vases, plates, bowls and dishes. Another typical imperfection you will find is a chip. This will vary from what I call 'pin-holes', meaning nicks in the glass that are the size of the point of a pin, through to a chip, of indeterminate size. A chip can appear in the form of an indentation and/or a slither on the surface of the body, and can vary in size and depth. On some pieces whole chunks of glass may have come off. In many cases pieces with such damage can be made to look perfect, depending on the size and position of the damage, by expert polishing or grinding, even when large chunks are missing.

Cracks can occur in two forms. The cooling crack occurs during manufacture: the edges are smooth and fall in but do not generally go into the body, your finger nail falling into the crevice. These have occurred due to some projection from the mould, the molten glass forming a layer over it. Because they do not go into the body they will not get any worse, unlike a fracture crack or 'feather crack', which can be caused by a knock or a sudden change in temperature. These cracks are usually all too visible and can vary in depth, angle and length. 'Feather' cracks, however, can be very difficult to spot, needing close examination and the right method to find them. Internal cracks will only ever get worse with variations in temperature.

Unsightly lines in the mould can also occur, as will bubbles and detritus. In the main these are acceptable, but where they occur and how noticeable they are is important; after all you don't want a wavy accidental moulded line or small bubble acrsss the face of a figure or animal. An open bubble can also put off many buyers or collectors. You can also find that the thickness of the walls of, for example, a vase or bowl may not be the same due to the process of manufacture, and not always through later alterations.

Several designs were made using 'cased' glass, which could add an opaque effect to coloured translucent glass. This effect could be achieved using two layers of glass, an inner opaque layer with a coloured gather of glass on top or a triple layer with an opaque layer between two coloured or clear layers of glass. A quick way of identifying this method is to look down on the rim of the vessel, where the separate layers of glass are clearly visible.

Staining or patina colouring on glass was often used by Lalique, creating bold contrasting matt grounds in a variety of colours, more subtly to give detail to a delicate moulded pattern. The technique, used quite extensively during the early period by Lalique, involved coating or dipping the item into a coloured enamel solution, the raised part of the surface moulding then being wiped with a cloth, leaving the recesses holding the enamel. The enamel would then be fixed to the glass by firing at a low temperature in a muffle kiln. Contemporary pieces which have had artificial patina added to them are very thin, transparent and powdery by comparison, usually being a watercolour based-solution.

A more permanent and solid use of creating a surface staining was to paint a powdered enamel mixed with a binder onto the glass before firing. This created a thicker opaque layer of colour that fused with the glass, resulting in a hard baked surface. Today you may come across recently altered pieces that look like the baked enamel pieces. These you will find have a far softer feel and look to the surface, being thinly applied and allowed to harden.

How to look
Armed with the knowledge of what you might find, it is now time to find out how to look at and handle the objects, and more importantly how to become familiar with spotting alterations that have occurred to pieces over the years.

The initial approach to either a single piece or a collection of Lalique can be very informative. From a reasonable distance you can now start to assess the object by looking at the colour effect. If opalescent, how strong or deep is the tint and does it look aesthetically pleasing? If the whole body has been tinted, how deep is the colour? The effect of the frosted surface, often contrasted with clear areas, can also vary. Hand staining, using a wash of colour enamel applied at the time of manufacture to heighten the background and enrich the design, usually becomes very faded with time and use. Today you will find many such pieces, but you will also inevitably come across examples with recently added artificial staining, which is far thinner and more transparent in effect, with a dull lifeless look.

Is the piece straight? This is particularly relevant for car mascots, paperweights and figures, which can often warp or sag during the cooling process, and is especially noticeable on objects with a slightly over-balanced centre of gravity such as, 'Victoria', Cinq Chevaux, Comete, Grand Libellule, Chrysis, Petite Libellule, etc. Also you may find that in many of the larger heavier vases warping and sagging can occur, so it would be as well to check that the vase is not leaning to one side.

Stoppers in scent bottles and decanters can often sit too high or low in the neck, either beause they are replacements or have had a chip ground out of the polished cone base that fits into the neck. Some stoppers have very pendulous extensions falling down almost the length of the body. It is often worth checking, from edge on, to see if the extensions are vertical. In most cases a slight adjustment of the stopper may well correct the angle, assuming of course that the stopper will move. It might be prudent to ask the vendor if the stopper can be extracted, and if so to ask them to do it; it might just save a very embarrassing moment.

Bowls and vases are two of the most popular types of ware produced by Lalique, if for no other reason than they make the ideal gift. Being functional objects they also came in for their fair share of damage. Over the years various things will have been modified on them to stop the owners cutting themselves or throwing away a sentimental wedding gift. The base of the bowls raised on three moulded feet, often forming the pattern, may well vary in height, having been polished to remove damage. Wherever an item is likely to have been knocked, you will find a chip, bruise or crack, at the same places you might find repairs and polishing.

The use of your sense of touch is just as important, if not more so, when assesssing the condition of a piece of Lalique. Familiarity with the quality and variety of surface textures of Lalique glass could save you hundreds of pounds. You need to be able to feel and appreciate subtle changes in texture, which, together with your eyes, will help to confirm any variations in the surface of the piece.

Running your fingers over the top edge of the rim of a vase, bowl, etc., and feel if it is flat or rounded. Which was it meant to be? Gently pinch the rim and move your fingers around the edge and you might feel a variation in the thickness. This might mean that the rim was chipped at some stage in its life and polished. This is not always totally detrimental; it merely suggests that the piece may have had an annoying chip. Don't forget that many pieces after they had been made were given a bevelled or polished edge, usually very small, on the outside edge of a rim, foot or mould line, to get rid of any sharp flakes of glass due to the method of manufacture. Variations in the thickness of the rim can also be caused by the method of manufacture: for example, the central plug might not have been aligned properly during the manufacturing process or the centrifuge could be fractionally out of true.

You can also run your fingers over a seemingly smooth surface and unexpectedly feel a depression or change of texture. This requires closer inspection and an adequate light source, such as a window. To examine the area properly, hold the piece up to the high at shoulder or head level.

There is another part of your finger that comes in very useful, whilst we are on the subject: your fingernails. Handy for detecting minor chips, more importantly fingernails and tips are extremely useful for finding sharp edges, especially where there aren't meant to be any, such as on the cascading water from the water vessels being carried by the maidens on the 'Danaide' vases.

Using light and shadow to pick up alterations to the glass surface is also very important. By holding a piece of Lalique glass at various heights, and manipulating it in front of a light source, you can use the refractory quality of the glass to detect any defects that might exist and also asses the strength of the opalescence, colour and quality of the staining. This is often the only way you can hope to find well-hidden defects such as 'feather cracks'. These can be found on any wares of various thickness, but they are more likely to occur in solid cast figures, mascots, table decorations, etc. Using the above method, the only way you will know the object has such a crack is by a sudden flash as you rotate the piece. It pays to rock the object to and fro, slowly, keeping your head still, gradually working your way around the object. If it is a flat or shallow curved object, then start on the top and repeat, looking at the reverse. If it is a vessel don't forget to look at the inside as well.

This all sounds as if it is going to involve a lot of time and effort, but the more often you pick up and handle pieces, the more it becomes a subconscious act, almost an involuntary act. Take it from me, having spent several years as an auction room cataloguer, looking at between 300 to 500 objects a week, you become only too aware of where to look for damage. But you can only acquire such skills by handling pieces. Preferably a few hundred.

While your eyes are looking for any flashes, your hands can be searching for a variety of things: irregular or slightly undulating patches on what should be a smooth surface, or sharp edges on what should be a smooth curved ridge. By letting the pads of your fingers gently slide over the surface of the body you will be able to pick up the slightest variation/depression in what should be an even surface. A frosted surface will become gritty and irregular where a deep surface scratch once was. The raised beading on an Oursin (sea urchin) vase or prominent studs of the Rampillon vase might seem flatter than the ones on either side. If you happen to have a piece of glass near to you, whether Lalique or not, pick it up and have a go. Now try closing your eyes and let your fingers explore inside and outside the piece. With the thumb and forefinger placed either side of the rim feel the thickness.

You may also come across objects that are not what they appear to be: a wall-light fitting made from half a bowl, a ceiling light shade or 'plafonnier' from a bowl never intended for the purpose, a brooch made from the side panel of a scent bottle, etc. The range of completely made-up items, using heavily damaged pieces in the hope of salvaging some return, is surprisingly large and ever more inventive. The fun is being able to spot the right from the wrong and the good from the indifferent.

I am not saying that you have to know all of the above before you can even start to look at an object, or that you will always find something wrong. There are plenty of pieces of Lalique on the market and in people's collections that have very few, if any, defects; but at least if you know what to look for and how to find any faults or alterations, you won't get any unexpected surprises later on or pay far more than the object was truly worth. By developing these skills you can quickly become very competent in assessing objects. In time you will have the skills and knowledge of some of the leading experts and collectors of Lalique glass.

*A rare **Bouchon Fleurs de Pommier** scent bottle, 13.5cm high, with pink-staining on a clear and frosted design.£7000/$10,850 in pink staining, £4800/$7440 blue staining.*

*A rare **Leurs Ames** clear and sepia-stained scent bottle, 13cm high. The tiara-shaped stopper has occasionally been matched to a wrong bottle. c£9000/$15500.*

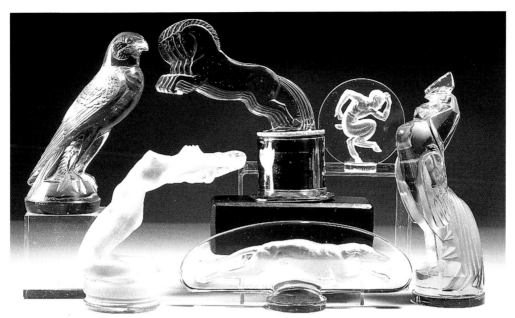

Left to right: **Faucon**, *15.2cm high, £800/$1240.* **Cinq Chevaux**, *15cm high, £3500/$5425.* **Faune**, *15.2cm high, £500/$775.* **Coq Houdan**, *20cm high, £1000/$1550.* **Chrysis**, *14.5cm high, £1200/$1860. Look out for the less elegant British Red Ashay version of Chrysis which has a square base, the figure being more upright and with both elbows raised.* **Lévrier**, *19.8cm long, £1000/$1550.*

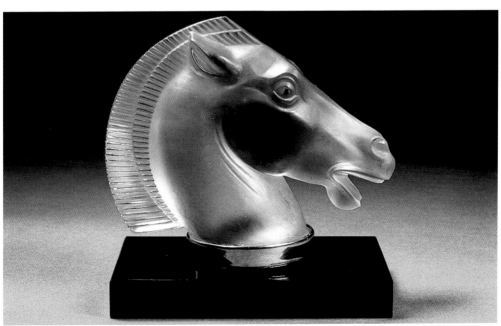

A **Longchamps** *frosted glass car mascot, 12.5cm high, as a paperweight. There are two versions of this model, another illustrated in the 1925 catalogue having a fuller main with broader single repeated cuts and a more angular and wider step to the base, £1600/$2480. Another version,* **Epsom**, *was made by Red Ashay in Britain with a forward thrusting head.*

*A pair of **Cariatide** clear and frosted candlesticks, 28cm high, with grey-staining. The obvious places to check for damage and/or alterations are the most vulnerable: the foot and the drip-pans. c£10,500/$18,750.*

Left to right. Top: **Le Baiser du Faune**, 15.5cm, £600/$930. **Semis des Fleurs**, 7cm, £500/$775. **Cigalia**, with box, 13cm£1200/$1860. **Althea**, 10cm, £800/$1240. Bottom: **Mousseline** with box, 9.2cm, £600/$930. **Le Corail Rouge**, with box, 10.5cm, £7000/$10,850. **Tzigane** with box, 14.3cm, £400/$620.

This **Margaret** vase, 23cm high, with sepia-stained and frosted handles on a clear glass body, is a very impressive piece, showing the technical mastery Lalique developed. c£5500/$9000

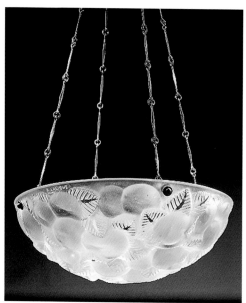

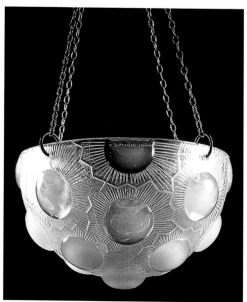

A *Lausanne* clear, frosted and amber plafonnier, 38cm diam. It is always advisable to check the drilled holes for cracking and chips. c£750/$1500.

A *Soleil* opalescent and frosted plafonnier, 30.5cm diam. The rings and chain are later additions, although they do make it easier to check the drilled holes for damage. c£1400/$2500

Left to right: A *Lutteurs* pale sepia-stained, frosted and clear glass vase, 13.5cm high. An opalescent and frosted statuette of *Suzanne*, 23cm high, with an unfortunate internal crack to the front leg, £4000/$6200. A frosted and opalescent statuette of *Sirene*, 10cm high (make sure the sides of the base are vertical) £2000/$3100. A frosted *Figurine avec Guirlande de Fruites* with sepia-staining, 21cm high.

*A pale amethyst and frosted **Vitesse** car mascot, 18.2cm high. c£3200/$5000.*

Left to right. Top: **Chypre**, *6.7cm, £700/$1085.* **Poesie**, *14.5cm,£2500/$3875.* **Eau de Lubin**, *14cm,£350/$545.* **Relief**, *17cm, £350/$465.* **Roncier**, *11.5cm, £1500/$2325.* **Fleurs Concaves**, *13cm, £600/$930. Bottom:* **Figurines Drapées Dansant**, *9cm, £500/$775.* **Epines**, *11cm, £350/$545.* **La Belle Saison**, *14cm, £1200/$1860.* **Bouquet de Faunes**, *10cm, £600/$930.* **Sans Adieu**, *13.5cm, £750/$1165.* **Figurines et Guirlandes**, *7cm, £300/$465.*

Left to right. Top: **Amphitrite**, *9.5cm, £1500/$2325.* **Cruciforme Fleurs**, *10cm, £1600/$2480.* **Panier de Roses**, *10cm, £1400/$2170.* **Clamart**, *11.3cm, £500/$775.* **Violette**, *8cm, £2000/$3100.* **Roses**, *10.5cm, £1500/$2325.* **Coeur Joie**, *15cm, £300/$465. Middle:* **Le Jade**, *8.2cm, £1800/$2790.* **Telline**, *9.6cm, £800/$1240. Bottom:* **Ambre**, *13cm, £1100/$1705.* **Vers le Jour**, *10.7cm, £1000/$1550.* **Poesie**, *14.5cm, £1500/$2325 (depending on colour).* **Olives**, *11.5cm, £800/$1240.* **Lentiles**, *5cm, £400/$620.* **Le Temp des Lilas**, *8.5cm, £250/$380.* **Vers Toi,** *5.1cm, £300/$465.*

*A **Bales** black enamelled and frosted vase, 26.7cm high. Note the hard and reflective enamelling, baked onto the body. c£6500/$11500.*

*A **Frise Aigles** frosted vase with blue-staining, 21cm high. c£3500/$6250*

*A **Salmonides** blue-stained and frosted vase, 29cm high, £5000/$7750.*

*A **Satyr** clear and frosted carafe with sepia-staining, 24cm high. The rim in this case has been slightly reduced. £600/$930.*

A pale blue and frosted **Au Coeur des Calices** *scent bottle with reduced wings on the bee stopper, 6cm high. £1200/$1860 in this condition – £6000/$9300 perfect.*

A **Bacchantes** *opalescent and frosted vase, with blue-staining, 25cm high. £6000/$9300 for this one although they can get up to the £10,000/$15,500 mark depending on the opalescence and staining.*

Left to right.
Top: **Phalènes**, *39cm diam, £2000/$3100;* **Flora-Bella**, *39cm diam. £1600/$2480; Bottom:* **Roscoff**, *35.5cm diam, £800/$1240;* **Martigues**, *36cm diam, £1200/$1860;* **Poissons** *vase, 24cm high, 32400/$3720.*

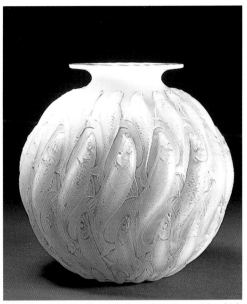

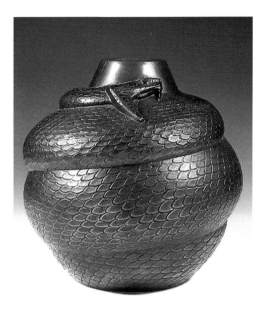

A *Marisa* opalescent blue-stained and frosted vase, 24cm high. £3700/$5735.

A *Serpent* grey-stained frosted vase, 24.8cm high. c£4500/$7900.

This *Eglantines* circular mirror, 43cm diam., has foil-backed glass, stained in grey. The sections are held in place by silvered brass mounts. £6500/$10,075

A rare turquoise blue and frosted *Tourbillons* vase, 20cm high. Regarded by most collectors as one of his most impressive mass production designs, representative of the Art Deco style of the period and showing great technical skill. c£26,000/$45,750.

*Detail of a rare frosted and cased emerald green **Gros Scarabees**, 30cm high.*

*A **Roitelets** clear and frosted clock, 19cm high, heightened with sepia-staining. The wing tips are certainly worthy of close inspection, £2800/$4340.*

*Two **Faucon** amethyst car mascots, 16cm, one with a London Breves Gallery mount. Should two such mascots be found at the same time, the collector has the rare opportunity to study any differences, whether they collect them or not. When mounted these often received damage to the base, being slightly awkward. Left: £1500/$2325; Right: £1200/$1860.*

*A **Victoire** amethyst-tinted frosted and clear car mascot, 25.5cm long. Representative of movement, speed and strength, these were very popular, with plenty about today. Look out for the British Red Ashay copies, which usually have frown and neck lines and a smaller mouth. c£5500/$9500.*

44

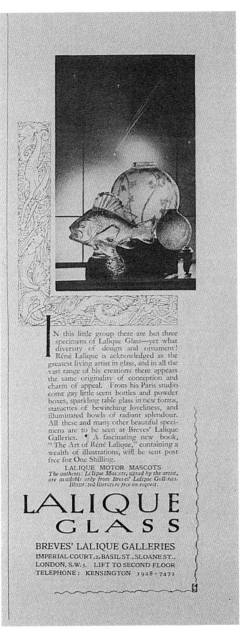

N this little group there are but three specimens of Lalique Glass—yet what diversity of design and ornament! Réné Lalique is acknowledged as the greatest living artist in glass, and in all the vast range of his creations there appears the same originality of conception and charm of appeal. From his Paris studio come gay little scent bottles and powder boxes, sparkling table glass in new forms, statuettes of bewitching loveliness, and illuminated bowls of radiant splendour. All these and many other beautiful specimens are to be seen at Breves' Lalique Galleries. ¶ A fascinating new book, "The Art of Réné Lalique," containing a wealth of illustrations, will be sent post free for One Shilling.

LALIQUE MOTOR MASCOTS
The authentic Lalique Mascots, signed by the artist, are available only from Breves' Lalique Galleries. Illustrated literature free on request.

LALIQUE
GLASS

BREVES' LALIQUE GALLERIES
IMPERIAL COURT, 2, BASIL ST., SLOANE ST.,
LONDON, S.W.3. LIFT TO SECOND FLOOR
TELEPHONE : KENSINGTON 1928 - 7471

The Firebird Screen, illustrated above, is illuminated from the base by a soft light which lends an almost ethereal beauty to the figure.

L ALIQUE GLASS is the product of a master who is not content to follow traditional forms, for the aim of Réné Lalique is to discover new uses and invent new themes. His productions include not only vases, statuettes and innumerable beautiful objects of original design, but lighting pieces which achieve effects never before realised. At the 1928 Paris Salon Exhibition, Lalique presented a modern interior in which every decorative feature was designed in glass. This remarkable exhibit will shortly be re-erected at Breves' Lalique Galleries.

An interesting new book, "The Art of Réné Lalique," with illustrations of a wide variety of examples, will be sent post free for one shilling.

LALIQUE
GLASS

BREVES' LALIQUE GALLERIES
IMPERIAL COURT, 2, BASIL ST., SLOANE ST.
LONDON, S.W.1 LIFT TO SECOND FLOOR
TELEPHONE: KENSINGTON 1928 - 7471

LXXX

A Breves' Lalique Gallery advertisement from The Connoisseur, March 1929. An interesting note at the bottom of the script reads 'The authentic Lalique Mascots, signed by the artists, are available only from Breves' Lalique Galleries. Illustrated literature free on request'. This would seem to indicate that the gallery was having problems with imitators, no doubt referring to the items made by the British firm Red Ashay.

A Breves' Lalique Gallery advertisement from The Connoisseur, April 1929, which mentions the modern interior room exhibited by Lalique at the 1928 Paris Salon Exhibition, 'shortly [to] be re-erected at the Breves Lalique Galleries'.

Left to right. Top: **Mures**, *19cm high, £1700/$2635.* **Armorique cased glass**, *22cm high, £3000/$4650.* **Prunes**, *17.8cm high, £3000/$4650. Middle:* **Corinthe**, *18.5cm high, £600/$930.* **Nivernais**, *17cm high, £700/$1085.* **Caudebec** *14.5cm high, £600/$930.* **Champagne**, *16.5cm high, £550/$855. Bottom:* **Monnaie du Pape cased glass**, *23.5cm high, £1500/$2325.* **Druide**, *18cm high, £500/$775.* **Font-Romeu**, *22.4cm high, £600/$930.* **Ferrières**, *16.5cm high, $500/$775.*

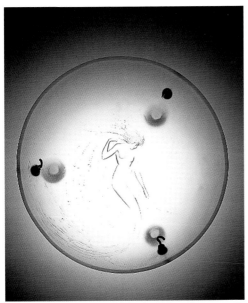

*A **Trepied Sirene** opalescent plafonnier 35.5cm. Here we see the adaptation of what was originally a dish, indicated by the three feet, of little use in mid air! £2000/$3100.*

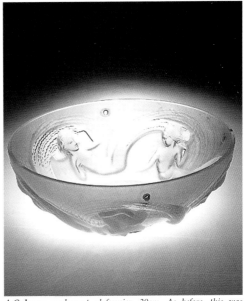

*A **Calypso** opalescent plafonnier, 30cm. As before, this was designed to be a bowl, the base having a foot and a plain centre, unlike a true ceiling shade. £2000/$3100.*

*A fake Lalique **Bacchantes** vase. The colour is immediately suspect, and the texture of the surface, weight and brilliance of the glass all add to the argument against this piece.*

*A **Inséparables** clock stand with movement, 11cm high. This is quite a common piece, being a very popular gift, although the quality of the opalescence and face of the dial vary considerably, as do the prices. The repeated design on the dial is particularly sought after. c£1760/$3100.*

*Left: This **Cyclamen** scent bottle, 13.8cm, made for Coty with slight green-staining, certainly doesn't look right. Imagine the stopper taken out, what are you left with? No neck what so ever. The neck should cover the clear section of the stopper with a flange over half the diameter of the disc of the stopper.*

*Right: A clear glass **Troi Guêpes** scent bottle, 12cm high, with sepia-staining. This is quite a rare piece, but even so look out for damage to the base wasps and the ends of their wings, these are particularly vulnerable.*

*A **Vitesse** amethyst-tinted frosted model of a figure, 18.5cm high. This figure has for some reason been glued to another piece of glass, possibly later adapted as a paperweight. c£2000/$3500.*

*This model of **Vitesse** with its strong opalescence is far rarer. It shows the marked difference achieved when compared to the pale tinted and frosted version (left). c£8250/$14500.*

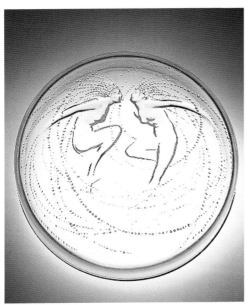

*A **Deux Sirenes** opalescent powder box, 25.5cm diam. c£1870/$3300.*

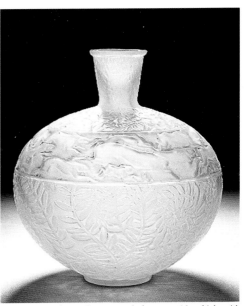

***Lièvres** is another opalescent cased glass vase, 16cm high, with blue-staining, having the same consistent colouring effect. c£880/$1550.*

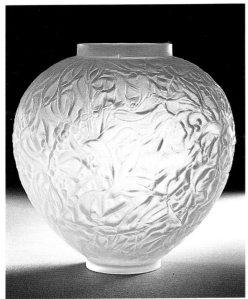

*This **Gui** opalescent vase, 17cm high, with traces of blue-staining has a consistent overall satin opalescence created by the use of 'cased' glass. c£530/$900.*

*The detail of the **Gui** vase, looking down at the rim, shows the opalescent layer of glass sandwiched between clear glass.*

A group of powder boxes can form an ideal beginner's collection, generally selling for between £300–£700/$465–$1085. Be sure to check the bottom edge of the lid, the inner rim and the outer edges of the base. Left to right. Top: **Figurines et Guirlandes**, *10cm diam.* **Roger**, *13.2cm diam.* **Dahlia bôite No.2**, *11.5cm diam. Middle:* **Emaliane**, *9cm diam.* **Quatre Flacons**, *14cm diam.* **Fontainebleau**, *8.5cm diam. Bottom:* **Meudon**, *8.5cm diam.* **Chrysanthème**, *8.5cm diam.* **Marguerites**, *8cm diam.*

*These two **Danaides**, 18.5cm high, opalescent vases show a variation in height, (compare the top rims and width of the base). The vase on the right has a very damaged foot. A third vase (on page 61) also shows a marked reduction in the width of the foot, such discrepancies altering the value only a little.*

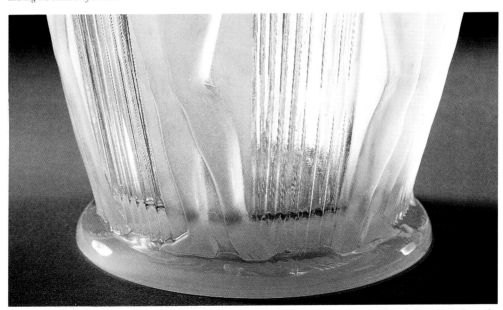

*This detail of a **Danaides** vase shows grinding marks to the falling water on the four right-hand vertical flutes in line with the knee. Also notice a flat spot area caused by polishing, highlighted in the rectangular reflection on the base by the feet of the right-hand woman.*

A moulded and frosted glass panel by Hailwood and Ackroyd of Morley, near Leeds, 1931. 38.7cm long.

*A **Sabino** moulded and frosted blue glass vase. 1930s.*

*A **Martigues** opalescent dish, 36.5cm diam, £1800/$2790.*

Left to right. Top: **Lièvres**, *16cm high, £550/$855.* **Villard**, *32cm wide, £1400/$2170.* **Perles**, *12cm high, £500/$775. Middle:* **Gimperaux**, *21cm high, £800/$1240.* **Beautreillis**, *14.5cm high, 3800/$1240.* **Danaides**, *18.5cm high, £600/$930. Bottom:* **Bluets**, *16cm high, £1200/$1860.* **Druide**, *17.5cm high, £800/$1240.* **Dentele**, *19cm high, £600/$930.*

Left to right. Top: **Honfleur**, *14cm high, £400/$620.* **Laurier**, *17.5cm high, £600/$930. Middle:* **Danaides**, *18.5cm high, £1500/$2325 (its all in the colour).* **Palmes**, *11.5cm high, £700/$1085.* **Plumes**, *21.5cm high, £800/$1240. Bottom:* **Rampillon**, *12.7cm, £350/$545.* **Oursin**, *18cm high, £700/$1085.* **Raisins**, *15.8cm high, £400/$620.*

What looks like a bowl with concentric beaded bands started out life as a vase, **Graines**, *and was twice the height at almost 20cm high. The top row of beading would have been circular, above which was a wide flared clear glass neck.*

A **Montmorency** *opalescent vase, 20cm high, with blue-staining. The variation in depth of relief on this heavy vase is often the cause of internal cracks during the cooling process. c£2700/$4750.*

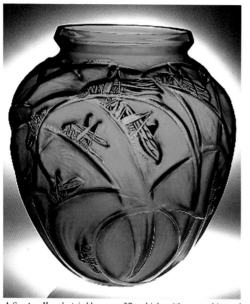

A **Sauterelles** electric blue vase, 27cm high, with some white and green-staining. An example of the rare and expensive end of Lalique. c£6400/$1125.

A **Biskra** opalescent vase, 28.5cm high, £1600/$2480.

These two **Cerices** opalescent glass vases, 20cm high, tell their own story. The yellow-based body (left) having a rougher looking flared neck, whilst the one of the right has a crisp satin finish and blue-staining. Left: c£930/$1635; Right £2600/$4570.

*This group of six **Ceylan** vases, approx. 24cm high, shows the variations that occur and how popular they were. The most sought after being the bottom centre, with its strong opalescence next the one on the left, with strong staining, followed by the top centre and bottom right, the last two being flatter in tone and lacking the staining. You can also see a variation in the depth on the base, although as with the Danaides this makes little difference when it comes to value. From top left: c£1760/$3095; c£1980/$3480; c£1430/$2500. Bottom left: c£2090/$3675; c£2090/$3675; c£1980/$3480.*

*Four **Monnaie du Pape** vases 23cm and 23.5cm high giving an idea of some of the colour variations used. Top vases are both cased glass. Note the chip on the rim of top left and the essential mould line and cased ring on the rim of top right. Bottom left is a dark frosted topaz, with possibly some white-staining, and bottom right, a dark amber frosted body raised on a bronze base. The picture on page 47 shows another cased opalescent vase. From top left: £990/$1535 with chip; £1500/$2325; £1300/$2015; £3000/$4650.*

*This **Suzanne**, 23cm high, figure would appear to be extremely sought after, being amber coloured and with the right hand. Unfortunately it has a serious deep crack to the front of the base. A realistic price for this would be in the mid to high hundreds compared to the mid to high thousands.*

An **Actinia** opalescent vase, 22cm high. This must be treated with caution, as there should be a 2mm clear band above the design. Have fun checking the serrated patterning. £1200/$1860.

A **Comètes** clear and frosted vase, 28cm high. The vulnerable parts are the starburst heads and tails. c£1000/$1600.

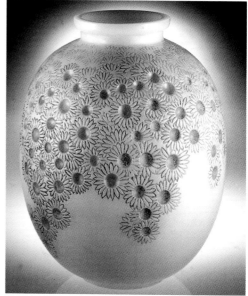

An **Yvelines** clear and frosted vase, 19.5cm high. The handles were probably applied after the body had been blown. c£1200/$2110.

The **Marguerites** frosted cased white glass vase with brown enamelling, 21cm high, is one of a small number of vases made using opaque white glass. The enamelling was also carried out in blue and black. c£1500/$2650.

Ambre (introduced in 1912) for D'Orsay. There are three versions of this bottle, all 13cm high, the others both being clear and frosted, but one has hand-stained figures. There is another clearer illustration on page 78 (£2,000/$3,000)

*This **Sauterelles** clear and frosted vase, 27cm high, with blue and green-staining has been converted to a table lamp. Many designs were converted in this way, some having the shade decorated in the same pattern. Unfortunately the drilled hole in the base will only detract from the value. c£1000/$1450.*

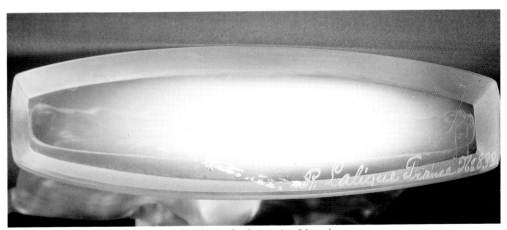

*A detail of the mark on **Suzanne** (introduced 1925). Notice also the intensity of the opalescence.*

59

*A **Borneo** clear and frosted vase, 23.8cm high. Make sure the dark red enamelling on the birds feels hard and looks glossy. c£1650/$2900.*

*An **Oran** opalescent vase, 26cm high, with blue-staining. Here again problems can occur during cooling due to the sudden change from high to low relief. c£5000/$8800.*

*This **Serpent** deep amber vase with staining, 25cm high, would be a much-prized find as the design of the coiled snake is quite beautiful. A strong light source is necessary to thoroughly check such deep colours. A rare and expensive piece, even rarer in violet. c£7000/$12,250.*

*Two **Sirenes** frosted brûle-parfums, 17cm high, one with grey-staining the other with sepia-staining. c£1600/$2800.*

*Top Row: **Saint-François** (introduced in 1930) in an opalescent glass, 17.5cm high. This is quite a common vase and appears with various levels or strengths of hand staining. (£500/$700); **Graines** (introduced in 1930) this is illustrated in greater detail on page 53 (£150/$200). In perfect condition it might have been worth between £1500/$2000); **Saint-Denis** (introduced in 1926) 17.5cm high. (£1000/$1500). Middle Row: **Senart** (introduced in 1934) in clear and frosted glass, 21cm high. This also appears with coloured hand staining and in various colours. (£300/$500); **Oursin** (introduced in 1935) in clear and frosted glass with the remains of a gray hand staining, 18cm high. (£300/$400); **Ajaccio** (introduced in 1938) in clear and frosted glass, 20.5cm high. (£600/$800). Bottom Row: **Silènes** (introduced in 1938) in a frosted and clear glass, 20.5cm high. (£300/$500); **Lièvres** (introduced in 1923), 16cm high. This is another of the distinctive cased opalescent glass vases with additional blue staining. (£800/$1000); **Beautreillis** (introduced in 1927) opalescent glass vase, 14.5cm high. (£500/$700).*

Left to right. Top: **Sorbier**, *5cm long.* **Gui**, *4.5cm high. Middle:* **Lys**, *5.5cm long. A white metal* **Chilean** *plaque, 6x4cm.* **Fougàres** *bracelet. Bottom:* **Deux Figurines Dos à Dos**, *5.5cm wide.*

Dentelé (introduced in 1912) heavily tinted gray glass, 19cm high. This is very similar to a perfume bottle designed for Volnay, Eau de Cologne aux Fruits (introduced in 1912) which had an additional stopper. (£400/$600).

Top row: **Cigalia** *(introduced in 1925) for Roger et Gallet, 18.5cm high. Four versions of this design were made for Roger et Gallet, the first three dating from 1923 being smaller and of squarer form. (£1200/$1800);* **Myosotis, Bouchon Figurine** *(introduced in 1928). This bottle is the smallest of three bottles, 23cm high, the others being 29cm and 26cm high, which are part of a set or garniture, another item being a circular box and cover. (£1200/$1400);* **Relief** *(introduced in 1924) for Forvil. This bottle can be found in four different sizes; 9cm, 14cm, 16cm and 21 cm high. (£200/$300). Middle Row:* **Calendal** *(introduced in 1923) for Molinard. This would have had a metal atomizer or vaporizer fitting, now shown with a temporary cap. (£200/$300);* **Worth** *(introduced in 1924) for Worth, 23cm high. There is a blue coloured version, in three different sizes 7.8cm, 13.5cm and 25.5cm high, as well as another similar with a star-studded globular body, although frosted, made for Worth called Dans la Nuit (introduced in 1924). (£100/$150);* **Bouquet de Faunes** *(introduced in 1925) for Guerlain. One of three sizes, 10cm, 11cm and 13.5cm high. (£200/$300). Bottom Row:* **Figurine** *(No:1) atomizer (introduced in 1924) for Marcus et Bardel, 9.5cm high. This model has sepia staining but there are also two other versions, one as a vaporizer and another as an atomizer which is some 15.5cm high, the latter being introduced in 1926. (£300/$500);* **Figurine et Guirlandes** *vaporizer (introduced in 1923) for Molinard. (£80/$120).*

Archers (introduced in 1921) in a clear and frosted glass, 26.3cm high. This comes in a variety of colourways, the price altering accordingly and just to give you an idea, in 1992 the same version of this vase sold for £1760/$2730 (including commission) and in 1996 another sold for £1725/$2675 (including commission).

Dahlias (introduced in 1923) with hand staining in brown and black enamelling, 12.5cm high. (£800/$1200).

Les Parfums de Coty (introduced between 1910-14) A boxed set of twelve bottles. There are at least two versions of this that you might come across, one having heart-shaped black and white paper labels on the bottles and another, seemingly more correct, with gilt embossed paper labels. The version seen here is worth in the region of £2000/$2500. One of the other versions which sold in December 1998 for £8625/$13,370.

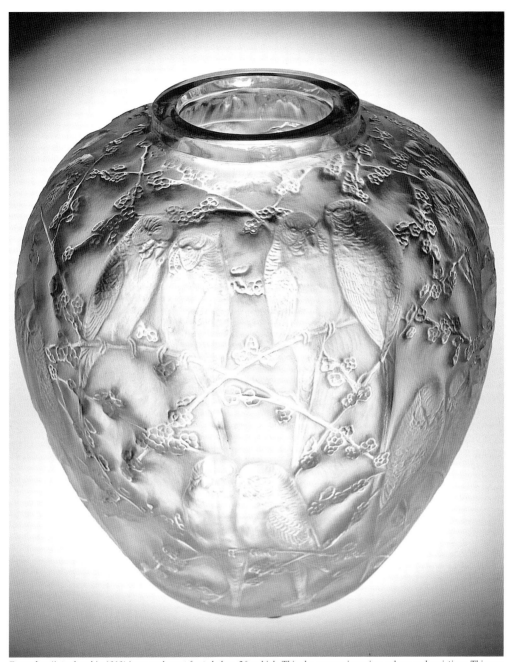

Perruches (introduced in 1919) in an opalescent frosted glass, 26cm high. This also appears in various colours and variations. This vase would have sold for £2200/$3410 in 1994 and today for the same price, having been down to £1200/$1860 in 1996. Two glass vases in electric blue sold for £12,000/$18,600 and £13,000/$20,150 in 1990, by 1992 you could not get £7000/$10,850 for one. The emerald green version sold for £4000/$6200 in 1989 and £8500/$13,175 in 1991. This vase should not be confused with its close cousin Alicante, which depicts three pairs of budgerigars heads and which have previously sold for £31,900/$49,445 in electric blue, at the height of the frenzied market in 1989, with a cased green glass version selling for around £16,000/$24,800, even today.

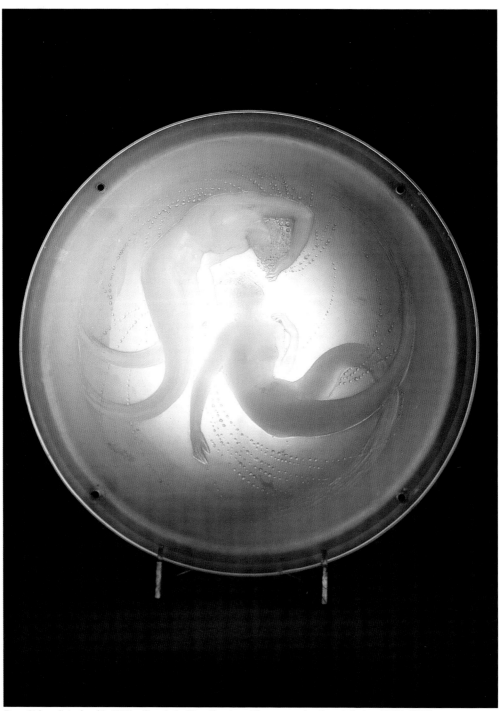

Deux Sirènes (introduced in 1921) ceiling shade, 39cm diameter, with a very good opalescent tinting. (£2500-$3500).

Archers (introduced in 1921) in a dark amber coloured glass, 26.5cm high. Here the price variation over a similar period has been quite different. In 1986 this vase would have sold for £3520/$5455, in 1988 for £3960/$6140, in 1994 there is a drop to £2750/$4265 and by the end of the year one could expect £2000/$2500. There are other versions with hand staining in brown, blue and red, all today at around £1700/$1900, as well as a quite unusual amber coloured glass version, £4000/$6200. Other colours include grey, green, electric blue and deep amber amongst others, these being some of the most sought after at around the £4000/$6200 level.

Ibis (introduced in 1934) with sepia hand-staining, 24.cm high. (£1500/$1800).

*A **Coq Nain** clear and frosted car mascot, 20.5cm high. This is the sort of item that is often polished, due to use. Check thoroughly, especially the beak, crest, toes, front, back and sides of the large tail feathers. c£2000/$3500*

*Two figures of **Suzanne**, 23cm high, and their rarer sister figure **Thais**, 21.5cm high. The opalescent figure of Suzanne is more collectable than the frosted figure, although both have their faults when compared to the picture on page 57. Notice the left hand, or lack of it, and the depth at the front of the base. The use of amber coloured glass for the Thais figure makes it a rare and sought after item. Suzanne (left) £900/$1395 in this condition; Suzanne (right) £1200/$1860 (a very good example can fetch up to £8000/$12,400); Thais (centre) £5000/$7750*

*Left to right. Top: **Canard**, 10cm diam, £300/$465. **Clos Saint-Odile**, 10.5cm high, £700/$1085. **Antilope**, 9cm high, £200/$310. **Canard**, 10.5cm diam, £300/$465. Second row: **Antilope**, grey, 8.5cm high, £300/$465. **Sanglier**, 6.5cm high, £500/$775. Third row: **Dindon**, 10.5cm diam, £150/$235. **Dindon**, 10cm high, £150/$235. Bottom: **Renard**, 10.5cm diam, £150/$235. This group shows animal and figure models, which could be fitted with a base to form a cendrier, each being formed separately. These can form the basis of an interesting and affordable collection. Sanglier could also be used as a car mascot, as illustrated in a Breves Gallery car mascot brochure.*

*An **Inséparables** opalescent, clear and frosted clock case and movement, 11cm high. This has particularly strong opalescence and a strikingly similar painted dial. c£2100/$3700.*

Vers Le Jour (introduced in 1926) for Worth. This was made in three sizes; 7.5cm, 13.5cm and 15.5cm high. This has a slight problem in that it has the wrong stopper, the correct one being a flat disc moulded with the same chevron design as found on the body. (£300/$600 for the illustrated one)

Ambre Antique (introduced in 1910) made for Coty with sepia hand staining, 15cm high. (£800/$1200 boxed, £700/$900without the box); *Cyclamen* (introduced in 1909) for Coty with hand staining, with its original box, 13.5cm high. This is not to be confused with another bottle for Coty called L'Aimant, made in 1912, which has a wide neck to the bottle and is not stained, and a later version of Cyclamen, 1912, which had no neck to the body, the stopper being wider at the base and fitting flush with the shoulder of the bottle. (Boxed £1200/$1800).

Bouchon Eucalyptus (introduced 1919) 13.5cm high, with a pale grey surface staining. This is one of those ones that you have to check for the length of the elongated leaves and width of mouth rim. In this case, everything appears to be in order. (£10,000/ $12,000).

Dans la Nuit (introduced in 1925) for Worth. This came in five different sizes; 8cm, 10cm, 12.5cm, 16cm and 24cm high. (£300/ $500 for the 16cm size)

Hélène (introduced in 1942) 14cm high, frosted and clear, this is part of a 'Garniture de toilette' with a similar taller bottle, 23cm high and a box, 8.5cm high. (£200/$300).

Vase Deux Anémones (introduced in 1935) 16cm high. Not to be confused with the decorative ornament based on the same shape and with the same name, also the same size, in which the two flowers were made separately (not as a stopper) (£400/$600).

Douze Figurine avec Bouchon Figurine vase and stopper (introduced in 1920) each 29.5cm high. (£1600/$1800).

Requête for Worth (*introduced in 1944*) *16cm high. This was made as a companion for smaller bottle for the same company seen on page 77 and can also be found in a 27.5cm high size.* (£600/$800).

Detail of **Duncan**, *flacon No:3 (introduced in 1931) 19cm high by 9cm wide. This is the type of thing that could be made-up into a brooch or some such item, so do beware.* (£1200/$1500).

Fleurs (introduced in 1925) for Colgate, 8.5cm high. (£700/$900).

Trois Guêpes *(introduced 1912) 12cm high. Just so that you can see what one of these looks like before, as in this case, and after, as in the sepia stained one.* (£4000/$5000).

Fougères (introduced in 1912) 9cm high, with green staining. The central oval panel of this bottle was also made as a medallion, unlike some of the others, such as Duncan, which can appear as a brooch or medallion (£10,000/$12,000).

Parfums (introduced in 1924) made for Forvil, with a sepia tint. This was made in three sizes 8cm, 10cm and 12cm. (£500/$700).

Requête for Worth (introduced in 1944) 8-9cm high. This was made as a companion for footed bottle for the same company seen on page 76 (£400/$600).

En Croisiere for Worth (introduced in 1935). This bottle comes in three different sizes, 4.5cm, 6.2cm and 8cm high. (£400/$600 for the 8cm size).

Capricornes (introduced in 1912) 8.5cm high. (£2500/$3500).

Ambre (introduced in 1912) for D'Orsay, 13cm high. A boxed bottle can be seen on page 59 (£1000/$2000).

Telline (introduced 1920) 10cm high, with a green colouring. This bottle can make between £700/$900, whilst an electric blue version can be worth £2200/$2600.

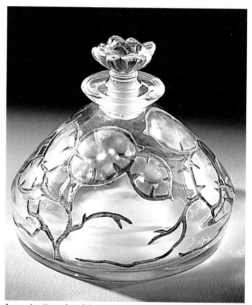

Lunaria (introduced in 1912) 8cm high with hand staining. (£3000/$4000).

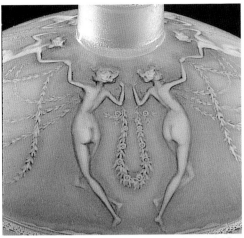

Trois Groupes de Deux Danseuses (introduced in 1912) 5.7cm high. (£12,000/$16,000).

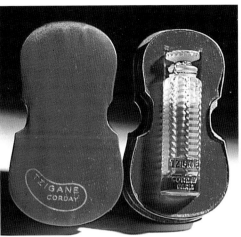

Tzigane (introduced in 1938) the only shape made for Corday. This bottle was made in four sizes; 11.5cm, 13.5cm, 17.5cm and 21cm high. (£800/$1000).

Le Succès (introduced in 1914) for D'Orsay in a frosted amethyst colouring, 9.5cm high. This should not be confused with Myosotis, Bouchon Figurine (introduced in 1928) which has a different body and figurative stopper, or for that matter Amphitrite (introduced in 1920) which has a snail-shell moulded body. If you are interested in buying one and see one, make sure it has the right stopper and has not been changed, after all they are very similar. (£1200/$1500).

Muguet (introduced in 1931) 10cm high. With a pale amethyst colouring this bottle is worth between £2500/$3500. Not to be confused with Clairefontaine (introduced in 1931) which has a globular clear glass body and far fewer, but more transparent, floral stems on the stopper.

La Sirène (introduced in 1912) for Burman, 10cm high. Notice that the bottle has never been opened and therefore still holds its original contents. There is also another taller version of this, 19cm high, made for Burman. (£6000/$8000).

Chypre (introduced in 1924) for Forvil. This bottle appears in various forms, as with so many other bottles made for perfume manufacturers and/or retailers. Forvil sold cased sets of three bottles during the 1920s. This bottle, with a red hand staining, would appear to have been sold by itself with its own cylindrical case. (£700/$900).

Hirondelles (introduced 1920) 9cm high. This has a particularly good colouring. (£2500/$3500).

Les Cinq Fleurs (introduced in 1926) for Forvil. The fact that the bottle has never been opened adds to the value of this particular one. They appear in five different sizes; 6.5cm, 8.5cm, 13cm, 15cm and 19.5cm. (£1000/$1500 for the illustrated one)

Where and What to Buy –
The Pros and Cons

Details of where you can find Lalique glass are just about everywhere either because of the recognition of the name or the total ignorance of it. Quite frankly you can start in a local garage sale, car boot fairs or charity shops, your local bric-à-brac/antique shops, antique fair or auction house, through to the major national auction houses, specialist Lalique shops and international auction houses. The lengths you are prepared to go to in the search for pieces is entirely up to you. The most obvious places to find what you are looking for are the specialist shops, auction houses and most antique fairs, which applies equally to most countries in the world.

In the UK the only regular annual sales devoted entirely to Lalique glass are held at Bonhams, Knightsbridge and Christie's, South Kensington, the latter recently deciding to hold two such specialist sales a year. Other auction houses in the UK, America, France, Australia, etc., might have an occasional special sale should a large private collection come up for auction. You can find out all about such sales from the weekly antique newspaper, the Antiques Trade Gazette, an essential read if you want to buy from an auction house. This is a vital tool for all dealers, helping them to keep one step ahead of those who are unaware of it.

The collector, whether a recent beginner or long-time servant, now has access to a completely computerised auction service, Thesaurus. This service inputs every item coming up for auction in the UK, from the humblest photocopied handout of the small provincial auction houses to the major auction room colour catalogues. As a subscriber you will be sent up-to-date computer print-outs of any Lalique coming up for sale, with all the necessary details. This is a service that can be provided anywhere in the UK and overseas.

It is certainly a good idea to see as many pieces as you can before you decide which type of object, style of design or features you want to start collecting. Your judgement should, more likely will, take into account not only the level of pricing you can afford but also the condition of the objects. Whether minor chips or missing chunks, would be acceptable to you or, and I use the word reservedly, only 'perfect' pieces. One of the most stunning little collections I have seen arranged the pieces amongst other objects or filled them with dried flowers, and some objects in natural light, others with spot-lighting, probably cost less than a single perfect mid-range Lalique vase, as all the objects were damaged.

For the beginner it is as well to start off by staying well within your budget, purchasing a few pieces, so that you can take a closer look at them at your leisure. Having gained more confidence in your ability to assess the pieces, you will then be better equipped to start developing the type of collection you have always wanted.

Exactly what to collect is then entirely up to you. Some of the most popular items include scent bottles, car mascots, vases, bowls, jewellery and cendriers. Being popular you might think that it would be better to stay clear of these areas and pick something else, and this is often a good idea. However, the only reason the above items are so popular is because there were plenty made and they still abound today. You could collect animal or figure subjects, powder boxes or brooches, floral patterns or wine glasses. Whatever your choice, and I'm sure you can come up with a few more types, having done your homework, the object is to have fun and to get pleasure from not only building up a collection but from the process of finding those objects.

All the time your aim should be, with just a little guidance and a lot of handling of pieces, to develop a knowledge that gives you an advantage. You will know when you have an advantage when you talk to a stall holder at an antique fair or a shop owner about a piece they are selling, and what they tell you is either what you knew already or inaccurate. There is nothing more satisfying than knowing what you are talking about, spotting a repair, finding a piece of jewellery made from a broken up scent bottle or a piece of cased glass priced as an ordinary piece of the same design.

Never forget that if you only handle a few dozen pieces and look at them in the right way, you will probably have seen more pieces of Lalique than the average local general antique dealer will in a year or more.
There is a wide selection of books available on the subject of Lalique, some specifically on certain objects like scent bottles, although most have mainly black and white illustrations. The one essential reference for any serious collector is Lalique Catalogue Raisonné by Felix Marcilhac. This has over 1000 pages containing over 3600 documented designs mostly illustrated with details of size, production date and colours available. If your French is up to par then you will certainly enjoy the 200 pages of text, as the book is only published in French and is rather costly. Another well-illustrated reference book is the 1981 reprinted copy of the Lalique catalogue for 1925, which has 1500 illustrations, again sadly only in black and white.

So what is the difference between buying from a shop, the fair or the auction house? All three venues have advantages and disadvantages. If you are only looking for certain specific pieces of Lalique via the auction houses, then you could receive dozens of catalogues with either nothing for you or when pieces are viewed not in the condition or with the right strength of colour you are looking for. Indeed much the same could be said of specialist shops and antique fairs; only the cost of the catalogues will certainly add up.

None of the three may have what you are particularly looking for, the right conditions in which to view pieces or necessarily the right price. But each has its positive side. You will possibly get a better price at the auction house than at a shop or fair, if only because a large percentage of the Lalique in auctions is bought by dealers who merely put the items in their shop, possibly after some modifications, with a profit margin added to the price they paid. Recently, however, there has been a growing trend for private buyers and collectors to buy more frequently at auction, notably from both the general and specialist Lalique sales, particularly those held at Christie's, South Kensington. But these are only general rules; sometimes a dealer has a request from a client which he/she will want to deliver, even if it means a reduced profit margin. Equally not all the pieces in an auction will necessarily have come from private sources; look out for the dagger mark next to the lot number.

The shop or fair may have a small proportion of items bought in directly from the public, which therefore means that they are fresh onto the market, missing out the auction. In a shop, specialist stall in an antique centre or even sometimes at an antique fair you have more time to hold and examine the piece you want. It also has a fixed price, which, through discussion can be reduced to a more amicable figure. If you want to think about the purchase you can return later, often arranging with the seller that they hold the item for an agreed period while you think about the purchase.

Knowing what conditions you are likely to find pieces in is also important. Repairs on glass are often made because the vendors assume that the buyer would prefer to have the piece they are looking for in a whole state, rather than having to get the repair work done themselves, the vendor either writing on the label or telling the customer about the repairs. But there are some vendors who, whether through ignorance or by design, sell repaired pieces without mentioning this fact and often for the price of a perfect piece. You are unlikely to find such pieces sold by a specialist glass or Lalique dealer, as they will want to keep your custom and build up a good relationship with you. However, never be too trusting; make sure you do your homework.

A Word about Buying at Auction

There is still a generally held view that buying from auction is complex and best left to those who know what they are doing. Quite frankly nothing could be simpler. If there are any such beliefs, then these are only perpetuated by those who wish to keep this service for themselves. Buying from an auction is probably the most rewarding and exciting experience for any collector, whether from your own local auction or a specialist Lalique sale.

Every auction house, whether national or provincial, has to have their own 'seller's terms', 'conditions of sale/business' and 'release agreement'. As every auction is a separate business, their conditions, however similar, are all different. By law all three have to be on display, pointed out to the seller or buyer, or printed on the client's receipt and/or in the sale catalogue, usually at the back. These terms are there for a reason, not just to protect the auction house and/or the seller but also to inform and help the seller or buyer to understand what is required of them should they wish to make use of the auction. These conditions must always be read. If nothing else they can be quite amusing. Always ask if you are not exactly sure what is entailed; after all they welcome your custom, without it they couldn't survive.

The only way to be completely satisfied about any object you might be interested in buying is to go and examine it for yourself. And I mean 'examine', not just look at. If this is difficult because of constraints on time or distance, then the next best thing is to ask for a 'written' condition report to be posted or faxed to you, making sure you allow enough time for the condition report to reach you. A verbal telephone condition is not the same thing. In any event, even if you have examined an object on a viewing day, the more prudent collector/ buyer might well still ask for a written condition report, as there can be little comeback if the item you view one day has gained an extra defect by the time you come to collect the piece, before you sign the release, having paid for it. Dozens of people will have picked up and put down the piece you might eventually buy, in between the time you viewed it and the time you come to collect your purchase.

When you arrive for the sale check to see if there are any saleroom notices; these will tell you of any subsequent alterations to the condition of items or withdrawn lots after the publication of the catalogue. If you are coming a long way for just one or two lots, it might be prudent to ring up and find out if they are still in the sale before you depart. This could save a wasted journey and a lot of disappointment. If everything is well then I would suggest checking as many of the lots as you can before the sale begins, making a final choice.

When the auction has something you are interested in it is sometimes not the best place to examine a piece, due to dim lighting, a feverish, crowded atmosphere or just through lack of time. You are also only given an estimated price, which can sometimes be very misleading. Come the auction, even with the best knowledge of what such a piece ought to fetch, there might be one or two other people who are willing to pay way over the usual price. Equally there may be insufficient interest in a piece, the item failing to reach the client's reserve and therefore remaining unsold. In this situation, however, all is not lost, as you can approach the auctioneer or an assistant and make an offer on the lot in question. If your offer is on or over the reserve, the auctioneer can agree the sale, but only if immediately after the sale. If it is lower than the reserve, then the auctioneer will ring and/or write to the client to see whether they would be willing to accept your offer or not. The disappointment of not acquiring the piece you want is often deflating, but it should be balanced against the extra knowledge and experience you have acquired in handling and holding the piece. It can all be put to good use in the future.

Now for a cautionary word. Always check your purchase(s) thoroughly before signing the release form and leaving the building. This area is often a cause of much friction between a client and the auction house. Not many people realise, until too late, that the release form you are signing is also a disclaimer that says you are satisfied that the object(s) you are about to sign for is(are) not only the object(s) that you have now paid for but that you are happy that the condition is the same as when you last examined the piece. Once the release is signed and you leave the building, that is often the end of the matter. The conditions of business printed on the reverse of the release form are for your benefit, as much to protect the auction house at the end of their responsibility for the item you have taken away. Although it should be said that no rule is ever necessarily hard and fast. In the event of a dispute, whilst the client may not always be right, most auction houses do like to have happy customers, and will usually come to some sort of agreement, in the hope that they will come back again.

Although the conditions are often in plain English, it is certainly worth while getting to understand them. Develop a checklist or routine, whatever suits you, that you can become familiar with, making sure that everything you need to do is done in the right way and in the right order, so that the whole experience is rewarding and positive. Never rush or become complacent about the routine you develop. You may arrive home with a cracked, chipped or missing piece of glass that was once fine, only to find that there is little you can do about it. 'Chalk it down to experience' is not exactly what you want to hear from your comforter when a costly error might have been avoidable.

Buying at auction can be very rewarding, but may also generate mixed results. The main aim of the auctioneer is to get as much as they can on behalf of the vendor, who has entrusted the sale of their item to the auctioneer for this purpose, and the higher the price realised the more profit the auctioneer makes.

When your lot comes up during the auction you can start your bidding; precisely when to start bidding will be gleaned by experience. It is often best to wait as the auctioneer may often want to start too high, dropping to a more reasonable start when there is no response from the audience. Always bear in mind the buyer's commission and VAT which will be added on top of the hammer price so stick to your previously agreed top bid.

In many auction houses today you have to register before the auction to get a bidding number, which you call out or hold up if successful. It is also useful for waving about to initially gain the auctioneer's attention. At smaller auctions you merely shout out a name if successful and a member of staff, or runner, will be sent to get your name and address, especially if you are unknown to the auctioneer.

During the auction you might have two problems. First, the length of time before your lot(s) comes up for sale. Do you sit through the sale or come back later? Second, the speed of the auctioneer. Too fast and they can make mistakes, failing to see a slightly slow bid and bringing the hammer down too soon or taking a fractionally quicker bid than yours, acknowledging only your second bid which may put you on the 'wrong foot', or bidding increment, even taking you over what you wanted to pay. Equally a slow auctioneer creates a slightly apathetic atmosphere, which leaves your concentration flagging and your mind wandering. A cramped stuffy room doesn't help either, causing some people, including seasoned dealers, to miss the item they had intended to bid for. This can only be learnt through experience. Auctions take a great deal of concentration, which in turn can make the experience quite satisfying. Draining if not. Whether you are successful or not the whole process can be added to your experience and learning of what is involved in building up your collection.

Buying At Auction

There have been some interesting developments in the world of Lalique of which the reader should be made aware.

I have just returned from viewing a collection of Lalique that is about to be offered for auction in New York (although not at one either of the two most well-known auction houses), with some 164 lots on offer. The only reason for mentioning this sale is that the cataloguing was so poor it only serves to reiterate and confirm the belief, that if you as a collector or seller want to start dealing or buying in Lalique then you really do need to educate yourself before throwing money away. Only the two or three major International auction houses and the leading International specialist Lalique dealers will be able to offer anything like an accurate and accountable description or assessment of a piece or collection of Lalique. The only way to establish any kind of understanding is to educate yourself, which fortunately is not as difficult as might be thought.

To highlight what I mean here are some of the disasters awaiting the unwary buyer in the sale I mentioned above. Of the pieces entered for auction the most immediate common problem was the number of pieces that had been later hand-stained.

How can you spot this problem? Well, you firstly need to acquaint yourself with original unaltered hand-staining by looking, as I have suggested above, at pieces in that occur in the main offices of the two leading International auction houses, if you can, and/or go to see and handle pieces in specialist shops or fairs. Once you are on the premises ask questions, listen to the answers and then once you've seen enough leave and inwardly digest. After repeating this a few times you will start to understand and appreciate what true hand-staining is. The recently added staining looks like it has been painted on with a stiff brush, more often than not leaving brush marks behind, but it's the consistency that gives it away. You will see a heavily powered looking ground rather like painting a wall with a roller. The original staining looks more like an extremely fine misting, leaving a smooth unbroken surface and consistent colouring, although with age and use you do get faded and paler areas caused by washing and gentle rubbing. Another feature of the recently stained pieces is that they use the wrong colours, often far too bright or bold.

Another problem with this particular sale was that of five pieces which mentioned black enamelling, three were wrong. True enamelled colouring will be very hard and smooth, with a consistence of thickness, both in colour and depth, it might even have the odd surface blemish caused by a tiny air bubble bursting on the surface in the heat of the flames. Enamel, after all, in the true meaning of the word, is a glass-like paste made of metal oxides equating to a pigmented glass. Recently cold-painted highlighting, as added to the three pieces referred to above, will often have an inconsistent brushed on look, it will be thin, often to the point of allowing light through, and as a consequence of being hand-painted have irregular edges. In an effort to make cold-painted pieces look more effective, i.e. like the original, several layers might be put down to give the appearance or a smooth, think enamel but it can still be scraped off. The cataloguing would have been nearer the mark had it read 'later added black cold-painted highlights in imitation of black enamelling'. Later painted imitation enamelling, be it black, violet, blue, etc, will usually be able to be scraped off with the edge of a finger nail because it has not been fired or annealed onto or into the surface of the glass.

Recent Market Developments

During 1998, the Lalique market began to move again with a number of significant markers that point the way to a renewed interest in this highly prized glassware. This after the market has been fairly static in terms of pricing, if anything erring on the declining side for the past few years.

Initially it was Phillips who started to hold specialist Lalique auctions in the late 1970s, followed by Christie's in their New York office. By the early 1980s both auction houses had given up the single sale catalogues leaving Bonhams to fill the gap, in 1985, with their special evening sales. As a development of this in the early 1990s, Bonhams started to hold 'Commercial Scent Bottle' sales. The late 1980s saw a tremendous leap in prices, as with so many other fields, and one that was not sustainable during the 1990s, the depressed economic conditions of the period having taken almost all of the wind out of the Lalique sails. Prices have taken a long time to reach what can be called a reasonable 'market level'. At the end of 1998 pieces of Lalique started to sell well again, following the return of some confidence into the market. When I say sell I mean that prices started to exceed expectations, at least for those lots that were in very good condition. It must be said that even during the seven year wilderness Lalique glass was selling at auction and through specialist dealers, although generally only pieces in perfect condition or rare and/or interesting examples. Christie's South Kensington entered the single Lalique catalogue sale fold in 1994. The results of this sale, also reflected in pieces sold through other auctions, proved that in the main it was the lower end of the market, around £300-£600, that had kept the general market alive, while the unusual, fine and rare pieces, perfect condition being paramount, could still find buyers when expectations were reasonable.

In March 1998 Christie's achieved a world record for a Lalique vase, $409,500 for the "Roses" cire perdue vase, followed in June by another world record, this time for a statuette, 'Standing Maiden', again a lost wax model, which sold in Sotheby's, New York, for $288,500. This was then followed by the highly successful sale of The Mary Lou and Glenn Utt Collection of Lalique Perfume Bottles and related wares at Sotheby's, New York, on the 5th December 1998. Of the one hundred and seventy-nine perfume bottles, including boxes and display signs, only twelve lots went unsold. The Mary Lou and Glenn Utt collection is one of the acknowledged major International scent bottle collections, from whence the book "Lalique Perfume Bottles", published by Crown publishers, New York, 1990, developed. Naturally there were some important rare bottles that sold extremely well, including; "Oreilles Épines" (introduced in 1912) which sold for $68,500; "Grace D'Orsay (introduced in 1914) reached $33,350; both "Lézards Oreilles" (introduced 1912) and "Six Danseuses (introduced in 1912) sold for $31,625. Seven more bottles sold for over $20,000 with a further nineteen selling for over $10,000. This leaves us with one hundred and thirty-eight bottles that could be said to have sold for a more reasonable price, certainly within the level of this book.

Fakes and Reproductions

In the past fifteen to twenty years interest in the works of Lalique has increased rapidly. Associated with the developing awareness has been a steady rise in prices for his work across all levels of production. At the height of the market, in 1989/90, prices of between £10000 to £20000 were not uncommon, with some pieces such as a pair of 'Cariatide' frosted and brown-stained table decorations, 29.75cm high (not unlike the candlesticks illustrated on page 33) selling for £23000 and an electric blue 'Alicante' vase, 25.5cm high, for £31900.

Since 1991 such elevated prices have slowed and even fallen backwards a little, due to market conditions. But this has only been true of the rarer and most sought after pieces; the wares in the middle and bottom section of the market have stayed steady and even increased, especially when fresh perfect examples have appeared on the market. Since the middle of 1994 there has been an upturn in confidence, with prices across the board gaining as a result.

All this has meant that it is certainly worthwhile for some people to make new fakes in the hope of catching out the unwary. It should be remembered, however, that it is only really worth taking the time and effort to fake something of high value and therefore an associated rarity. At the bottom end of the market the only problems you will come across in this area are the contemporary reproductions and copies of Lalique's work, some made quite openly in the same style, but using different subjects. Others copy the same designs of Lalique, but in a different type of glass and with poor quality moulding, made to cash in on the demand for such glass. Unfortunately over time many such pieces have gained various Lalique signatures.

Imitators such as Sabino, Hunebelle, Carillio, Verlys and in Britain Jobling and Red Ashay, were strongly influenced by the Lalique style, often using a similar quality glass, but are distinctively different in design and moulding quality. The Red Ashay company manufactured direct copies, such as a figure resembling 'Chrysis', (see page 35), and also produced a version of 'Victoire' often with a curve to the base of the hair at the back of the neck and with a smaller mouth. The quality of the glass used by Red Ashay was very different to that of Lalique, and seemingly caused various blemishes to the surface and wrinkle lines as a result of inexperienced manufacturing methods especially during cooling. Bohemian and Czechoslovakian press-moulded wares were intended to deceive but used a very different quality glass, being crisper and more brilliant, and are therefore are quite easy to spot.

There are outright fakes still being made today, possibly in Romania, of prestigious vases such as 'Bacchantes', although the colours used are not correct and the pieces are too heavy. Quite frankly you are quite unlikely to be fooled by any of the copies and reproductions once you have handled a few dozen pieces of the real thing and become familiar with the surface texture and look of the glass.

Anything that sells for reasonably large sums of money is bound to attract the interest of fakers and Lalique glass is no stranger in this field. Recently I was in one of the many Antique centers in New York, and spotted an extremely good-looking fake Lalique vase. It was made in imitation of a red 'Formose' globular vase but had a very bad base, which was the most easily recognisable 'wrong' feature of the vase, apart from the colour. The base was not finished off in anyway, merely being left with a thin flat foot, the appearance of which was very undulating and full of foreign impurities. After this was noticed the heavier mould lines and odd frosting became apparent. To his credit the seller was not trying to sell it as Lalique, although was certainly not offering to suggest that it definitely wasn't Lalique, rather leaving it to the buyer to make up their own mind. If someone buys the piece thinking it was Lalique they would have little recourse for a refund as it would fall to into the 'buyer beware' category.

The last recent development specifically related to Lalique concerns a court case which was resolved (sort of) in December 1998. This related to a collection of seventeen purple coloured car mascots that were all sold to the same buyer on the assurance of the specialist dealer that they were coloured through a process of irradiation by René Lalique in the 1920's. Various other experts in the fields of glass and technology stated that Lalique never mentioned in any of his archival material that he had actually carried out such a process. Added to this it was stated that the process of irradiation was, in the 1920s, not developed sufficiently to made it viable for such a process to have been carried out on Lalique's glass. It was suggested that such a process might have been carried out on the glass, which was original clear glass, as late as the 1970s. At the end of the day, the judge found that whilst the dealer had not been negligent, not being an expert in the irradiation process, that he had given his professional assurance to the buyer that the glass had been coloured by René Lalique, which had not been found to be the case. The judge therefore found for the buyer and ordered the dealer and his gallery to pay damages and the buyers costs. There are several things that can gleaned from this case but mainly that dealers will have to be more circumspect about asserting something that they are not sure about or that they know would be difficult to back up, if need be, later. The other issue is that they are plenty of other purple pieces of Lalique out there on the market so buyers will have beware.

Price Guide

The mention of the name 'Lalique' to any antique dealer, auctioneer or bric-à-brac shop owner will instantly prick up the ears and open the eyes, but the nature of the material can often cover up its true identity.

Certainly there are many who, once they have read the name on a piece of Lalique glass, would start to equate it with objects worth hundreds of pounds. There are also now several well-known and more common pieces that are quite recognisable due to publicity or through repeated illustration in annual price guides and the like. But what if the name has been obscured by the passage of time and constant wear and tear? Who would instantly spot rare or unusual coloured pieces with barely discernible or hidden markings? How many car mascots were glued to deep wooden bases, hiding any markings a long time ago in the recesses of the wood? How many antique dealers, auctioneers, etc., would then be able to instantly recognise these pieces?

I ask these questions as they illustrate just some of the ways, amongst many other examples, that I have seen and heard of Lalique glass being found. Promotion by auction houses and specialist dealers works on the principle that the more pieces you illustrate, the more likely you are to get a response from someone who has had exactly the same object sitting on their windowsill for years, and was previously unaware of its identity.

Most of us are aware that Lalique made vases, bowls, car mascots, scent bottles, some figures and a few clocks. But what of the mirrors, picture frames, decanters, water jugs, drinking glasses, candlesticks, inkwells, blotters, ashtrays, beaded jewellery? How many such objects have been hidden away in a draw or cupboard, perhaps moved to the spare room or have always been dismissed as 'Granny's vase', you know the one?

Only last year a housewife on her way home after shopping called into a charity shop, where she spotted a small globular red vase amongst other assorted drinking glasses. She quite happily parted with £1.50 and left the shop. This charity shop was situated amongst a hive of specialist antique shops. The vase was admired at home and placed on the windowsill, its identity still hidden. After two or three weeks when some friends had come round for a meal the piece was talked about and picked up. The scrawled script was then deciphered and sudden recognised. The next day the vase was taken to the local regional auction house, where its value was roughly assessed and it was duly sent to the main office in London for a specialist opinion. The piece was then correctly identified, valued and sold for over £900, falling within the expected estimate.

Judging the correct price can however be very tricky, and any assessment of a piece must take into account a whole variety of criteria, the most obvious being rarity, quality, colour and the all important condition. But don't forget, condition is a highly personal thing that if taken to extremes might mean that you only ever buy one or two mint condition pieces. With Lalique you might need to be a little more forgiving and open-minded. There are numerous permutations of the above criteria that alter the final assessment of a piece.

It has to be borne in mind that many designs were not decorated with anything other than a clear and frosted surface. Others could be opalescence, or coloured, cased or enamelled. Some pieces used just one of these and some designs a combination of them.

Not all the criteria in the following bands will necessarily fit or be relevant to each particular group of wares. They should be seen as rough guides used with particular relevance to the object you are interested in. As with any classification there will always be a few exceptions to any general guidelines.

Key to Price Guide

Band 1

Clear and frosted or poor opalescence. No staining. Several areas or single area of extensive damage. Several polishing marks to various depths. Known and relatively common design. Less sought after design

Band 2

Clear and frosted, good opalescence, coloured, cased, enamelled. Some staining in various colours. Minor damage or small repairs. Known design but less common. Sought after design

Band 3

Unusual or rare colouring (electric blue, red, black). Good staining in strong colours. Very little if any damage and no repairs. Known but rare design. Highly sought after

Band 1

Scent Bottles
Small   £60–£100/$100–$170
Medium   £100–£400/$170–$680
Large   £200–£400/$340–$680

Atomisers
Medium   £80–£120/$135–$205

Brûle-parfums
Large   £150–£250/$255–$425

Vases
Small   £150–£350/$255–$595
Medium   £250–£1000/$425–$1700
Large   £900–£1500/$1530–$2550

Bowls
Small   £100–£250/$170–$425
Medium   £150–£350/$255–$595
Large   £500–£800/$850–$1360

Dishes
Small   £80–£120/$135–$205
Medium   £120–£250/$205–$425
Large   £350–£650/$595–$1105

Animal Models
Small   £60–£150/$100–$255
Medium   £200–£350/$340–$595
Large   £500–£800/$850–$1360

Cendriers
No model attached   £60–£120/$135–$205
Model attached   £100–£180/$170–$305

Ceiling shades/Plafonniers
Medium   £300–£500/$510–$850
Large   £400–£700/$680–$1190

Band 2

£100–£500/$170–$850
£400–£800/$680–$1360
£400–£800/$680–$1360

£120–£350/$205–$595

£250–£650/$425–$1105

£350–£800/$595–$1360
£1000–£3000/$1700–$5100
£1500–£5000/$2550–$8500

£250–£450/$425–$765
£350–£850/$595–$1445
£800–£1500/$1360–$2550

£120–£250/$204–$425
£250–£850/$425–$1445
£650–£1500/$1105–$2550

£150–£450/$255–$765
£350–£60/$595–$1020
£800–£1500/$1360–$2550

£120.–£350/$250–$595
£180–£350/$305–$595

£500–£800/$850–$1500
£700–£2000/$1190–$3400

Band 3

£500–£3,500/$850–$5950
£800–£5,000/$1360–$8500
£800–£4,000/$1360–$6800

£350–£800/$595–$1360

£650–£2,500/$1105–$4250

£800–£3000/$1200–$5100
£3000–£5000/$5100–$8500
£5000–£30000/$8500–$51000

£450–£650/$765–$1105
£850–£2000/$1445–$3400
£1500–£4000/$2550–$6800

£250–£600/$425–$1020
£850–£2500/$1445–$4250
£1500–£4000/$2550–$6800

£450–£1500/$650–$2550
£600–£2500/$1020–$4250
£1500–£5000/$2550–$8500

£350–£1000/$595–$1700
£350–£1500/$595–$2550   .

£800–£1200/$1360–$2040
£2000–£15000/$3400–$25500

Mascots
Small   £300–£500/$510–$850
Medium   £500–£800/$850–$1360

Figures
Small   £120–£200/$205–$340
Medium   £250–£550/$425–$935
Large   £600–£900/$1020–$1530

Clocks
Medium   £200–£600/$340–$1020
Large   £2000–£4000/$3400–$6800

Jewellery
Brooches   £400–£700/$680–$1190
Pendants   £200–£500/$340–$850
Necklaces   £700–£900/$1190–$1530

Boxes
Small   £80–£120/$135–$205
Medium   £120–£250/$205–$425
Large   £400–£600/$680–$1020

Tableware
Wine glass   £60–£120/$100–$205
Decanter   £200–£300/$340–$510
Plates   £40–£80/$70–$140

Mirrors
Small hand   £150–£250/$255–$425
Large hand   £300–£600/$510–$1020
Wall   £800–£1500/$1440–$2550

Table Lamps
Large   £2000–£4000/$3400–$6800

£500–£800/$850–$1360
£800–£2500/$1360–$4250

£800–£1500/$1360–$2550
£2500–£7000/$4250–$11900

£200–£400/$340–$680
£550–£1000/$935–$1700
£900–£3000/$1530–$5100

£400–£900/$680–$1530
£1000–£4000/$1700–$6800
£3000–£12000/$5100–$20400

£600–£1000/$1020–$1700
£4000–£7000/$6800–$11900

£1000–£3000/$1700–$5100
£7000–£20000/$7000–$34000a

£700–£1200/$1190–$2040
£500–£900/$850–$1530
£900–£1500/$1530–$2550

£1200–£3000/$2040–$5100
£900–£2000/$1530–$3400
£1500–£6000/$2550–$10200

£120–£400/$205–$680
£250–£650/$425–$1105
£600–£900/$1020–$1530

£400–£1000/$680–$1700
£650–£2000/$1105–$3400
£900–£3000/$1530–$5100

£120–£250/$205–$425
£300–£500/$510–$850
£80–£120/$135–$205

£250–£500/$425–$850
£500–£900/$850–$1530
£120–£500/$205–$850

£250–£450/$425–$765
£600–£1000/$1020–$1700
£1500–£3000/$2550–$5100

£450–£800/$765–$1350
£1000–£5000/$1700–$8500
£3000–£10000/$5100–$17000

£4000–£8000/$6800–$13500

£8000–£18000/$13500–$30600

Marks

The one thing you are usually sure to find on a piece of Lalique glass is a trademark; although finding it can cause a few problems, either due to use or because of the nature of the mark itself.

Marks seem to play only a relatively minor part when it comes to collecting and the perceived value of a piece, the exception being when the mark has been added later, the inevitable result of remedial polishing and alteration of the glass. First and foremost in the collector's mind when approaching a piece of Lalique, is the design, the crispness of execution and quality of the colouring and condition.

Even the most ardent collectors of Lalique have failed to establish a specific date span for the various marks. Certain types of mark would appear to have been most used on methods of production, with moulded marks being generally used on pieces made by mechanical power presses, just as a full script signature, 'R Lalique France. No: 2', appears to have been used mostly on blown-glass pieces. Wheel-engraved marks were also used on blown-glass items. Many pieces, such as the 'Ceylan' or 'Danaides' vases for example, can have at least three different styles of mark. The choice of mark may well have been dictated by the available surface area on the piece.

Falsely applied marks, whether on pieces by Lalique or his imitators, are noticeably broken and irregular, showing a lack of smooth and steady line. The genuine marks were the responsibility of a deft professional craftsman employed at the Lalique glassworks, who had spent months if not years wielding the various tools of his craft purely for the purpose of marking thousands of pieces. This said, the method of application did vary: in the case of the engraved script marks the variations in graphic style from one engraver to another has often led to claims of supposed forgeries, when it can just as easily be due to the individual character of the engraver. Only by hands-on experience will you truly be able to assess the difference between a right piece and a wrong one.

Between 1921 and 1925 some designs, most noticeably bowls, were moulded with a raised 'VDA' monogram to commemorate the opening of the new 'Verrerie d'Alsace' glassworks. This was also the largest mark used by the factory, the others usually being small enough to fit onto the foot rim or bottom edge of the base. Even the stencilled or moulded marks found in the middle of the base are small in comparison to its surface area. Large lettering or wordy markings are likely to be wrong. The only normal additions to the 'R.

Lalique' mark you will find will include 'France' and sometimes a design number, for example 'No: 384'.

Scent bottles usually have an engraved number on the base, which should also be found on the base of the stopper, indicating that the two pieces were specifically made to fit each other, the stoppers and/or neck of the bottle being ground to form a tight fit. Another point worth mentioning concerning scent bottles is the growing use of imitation paper labels, both applied to the glass and hanging from the neck. These are usually hand-copied marks and will therefore differ in feel from the original printed labels. Also being hand-copied there is usually an inconsistency in the size of lettering.

Original stencilled marks should always have regular caps in the lettering and at the same place on each letter. The letters should be evenly spaced. Remember that a thin metal plate is normally used by industrial manufacturers with a view to the most efficient and cost-effective method of marking, the lettering being accurately punched out of the metal sheet. Imitation stencilled marks, in contrast, are often crudely cut out of thin metal, omitting complete letters and leaving no caps, with letters that are frequently very irregular both in height and spacing.

With the death of René Lalique the company ceased to use the letter 'R' before 'Lalique' in its marks. There are several pieces with limited space for a mark, such as scent bottles, brooches and jewellery, made prior to 1945 that also did not include the letter 'R' in front. On some occasions old moulds were used after 1945, that incorporated a moulded 'R. Lalique' mark, in particular on car mascots and one or two bowls and vases, although the use of a different quality glass after the war should make the difference quite apparent.

As has already been mentioned there is no better experience than handling as many pieces of Lalique as you can. Your eyes, sense of touch and visual memory are the collector's best assets, through which you will build up the most useful basic knowledge which you can build on for many years to come.

To be aware of some of the possible problems you might encounter will form a sound base from which you can then so out and start building up your own hands-on knowledge, developing your own personal criteria for developing your collection.

Moulded Marks

 Left shows an indistinct mark general due to a lack of pressure in the method of production.

The use of the extended 'L' is relatively uncommon, occurring on the base of larger scent bottles and vases.

FRANCE. This mark is the typical mark seen on bowls, mascots, figures, etc., and is usually quite crisp and clear. It also appears without the letter 'R' and sometimes 'France'.

The semi-circular mark occurs on the outside rim of ceiling shades, bowls, dishes, etc.

Stencilled Mark

R. I. AI.IQUE

FRANCE

Note the broken lines or caps necessary in the use of a stencil.

Etched Wheel Cut Mark

This mark is sometimes combined with an engraved number and may also appear on a piece which has a moulded mark.

Engraved Mark

R LALIQUE

Again this mark was used in combination with others, although appears to have been used mostly on pressed objects before 1930.

Script-Etched Marks

(a), (b) and (c) type marks were used mainly on smaller pieces and sometimes omitting the letter 'R' due to a lack of space. On wine glasses the mark can be found in a small circular form including the word 'France'. All these marks were used on a variety of wares from 1918 through to more recent times, although latterly without the 'R' (c). The broader version (d) can typically be found on blown-glass wares from the mid 1920s to the late 1930s.

R. Lalique

Script-etched mark (a)

R. Lalique France

Script-etched mark (b)

Script-etched mark (c) with script-etched mark (d) below.

Lalique on the Internet

As with other collectables today, there is plenty of information to be found on the Internet relating to Lalique, both in terms of items to buy, but more importantly, some good historical information and buying guidelines on some of the specialist Lalique web sites.

The most obvious site name, **www.lalique.com** is, naturally enough, taken and copyrighted by the current makers and vendors of Lalique glass/crystal. This site is extremely pleasant and easy to visit and browse around. Not surprisingly it is mostly dedicated to selling and promoting the commercial wares being made today and the promotion of the only Lalique Collectors Club in existence (unless you know differently!). The club, called the Lalique Society of America, was launched in April 1989, during those frenzied years when the 'old' was making astronomical prices and the 'new' acquired a new following as a consequence. The first Lalique magazine was meant to produce just two copies a year, as stated in the first Spring/Summer issue of 1989, but such was the popularity that in the following year four editions were brought out. Some ten years on, the Society, now called the Lalique Collectors Society, part of Lalique North America, Inc., has developed a very useful looking web site (above) with informative articles on the history and contemporary glasswares.

One notable Web site **tony@finesse-fine-art.com** by Tony Wraight (UK), is a good example of how a well thought out and informative dealers site can come across. Specifically about Lalique car mascots (not paperweights) there is a very interesting series of articles dealing with their history, rarity, colour, issues of damage, copies, fakes, etc. Due to a recent exhibition which toured parts of America you can also find interesting articles on Lalique such as the ones on the Smithsonian Magazine web site, the Lalique exhibition which had been held at the Cooper-Hewitt National Design Museum, New York, in 1998, having attracted record crowds.

Buying, and even selling Lalique on the Internet, is, however, a classic case of 'buyer beware' as is probably apparent by now. I have given an example of how difficult it is to assess Lalique, even when holding the pieces in your hands in the chapter "Buying at Auction, or anywhere else." Difficult but by no means impossible after some practice. Buying via the Internet, not being able to handle the pieces to judge the quality and colour of the opalescence, let alone consider the condition and merits of any piece with your own eyes, I would suggest is next to impossible. The same could well be said for many objects on offer on the Internet. Internet buying has only just begun and is almost certainly going to get a great deal busier, so what is the solution? It would appear that we, meaning those of us who would normally not buy anything without being able to handle, view and assess the objects to our own satisfaction, or expect those looking for us, specialist dealers and reputable auction house cataloguers, to have similarly acutely trained eyes and knowledge of how to assess objects, to have to change our way of thinking. It would appear that we might just have to accept pieces, hopefully of a lesser price, within a wider set of acceptable perameters.

Buying Lalique glass, indeed anything, on or via the Internet has another problem related to live on-line auctions. In this case, you are watching and listening to the auction as it happens, having arranged to be on-line to bid, by registering with the auction concerned and acquired a secret pin number. All you do is sit in front of your computer and listen out for the lot numbers that you are interested in and when your lots come up you start pressing the pre-arranged appropriate keys to make a bid. At least, this is what the live on-line auction providers and auction houses would have you believe. Having, during such an auction, sat right next to the computer terminal operator, whose job it is not only to relay the on-going bid increments for every single lot as fast as is humanly possible but also to then, and at the same time, to bid on behalf of the Internet bidder any bids he/she or indeed they might wish to leave, there are a few observations that should be pointed out. As you can probably imagine there are going to be some split second delays or indeed some seconds delay in physically typing in the incremental bids but that shouldn't really matter if the action in the room can be heard. The question I was asking myself at the time during this auction was, why do so many of the Internet bids and subsequent shouts from the computer terminal operator come in after the hammer has gone down, often a few seconds after? More often than not, the hammer came down in favour of the telephone bidder, let alone the bidder in the room.

Basically, the need to operate keys by both the Internet operator and the person bidding, added to the time delay in reacting to a clients bid in the auction room, executing the bid, can only make the whole process extremely slow. There is a compounded delay time with every operation, equating to something in the region of nine to twelve seconds by which time the auctioneer has either taken another bid and sold the lot. To correct the imbalance would require the auctioneer to make special dispensation for Internet bids, waiting something like ten to twenty seconds while the Internet client decides what to do. Multiply such an action even a few times for one lot would drag out the auction time considerably, the same action for many lots would bring the whole proceeding to a halt.

I would therefore suggest that Internet bidding, subject to technological advances, will remain the province of the weekly posted auction sites where all or at least much of bidding tends to take place in the last hour even half an hour of the items remaining time. Live bidding has too much 'human' involvement to make it more than a sideline attraction.

There are numerous on-line auction and dealers sites where you can buy Lalique glass and this is where various issues arise, but mostly one of authenticity. How one sorts out the financial and delivery aspects is another on-going Internet problem. Perhaps some of the most well known person to person auction sites at present are ebay, icollector, ArtNet, EHammer and Amazon. The Auction Channel is slightly different from the above in that it allows auction houses, such as Christie's South Kensington, Phillips and Bonhams, UK, to conduct auctions through their channel, buyers being able to have live-pictures and Internet links to the auction and can bid either by phone, using the star button or via the Internet.

The year 2000 saw a significant development amongst the major auction houses with a positive endorsement of the Internet and it's future within the auctionroom world. Sotheby's launched it's own dedicated site for the sale of items via the Internet with it's sothebys.com web site. Having sought out and signed up over 4000 of the world's leading dealers in the fine arts and antiques fields Internet sale for the first half of 2000 were £20.0 million/$31.0 million. By the end of 2000 there were over 5000 major international dealers signed up and on-line sales of £38.7 million/$60 million for the first year. The year also saw a rather abortive partnership with Amazon.com to sell the low end material on a site called Sothebys.Amazon.com which did not do as well as expected through lack of a recognised and established identity – such as Sotheby's, in the auction world.

That the Sothebys.com site has done as well as it has is due in the main to the company's reputation and history but mainly due to the importance of the 'Guarantee of Authenticity and Condition' which was one of the early promotional slogans. The criteria of authenticity and expertise and the associated guarantees and history of the company are what set the Internet auction site apart from all the other lesser sites and make it able to sell expensive items – a Gutenberg Bible for £31,200/$48,400, an Andy Warhol work on paper Gold and Silver Shoe for £40,810/$63,250, a rare Marklin first series tin plate battleship "HMS Resolution" for £28,815/$44,660 being some of the most interesting lots.

Buying Lalique from the Sotheby's Internet site would enable the buyer to have all the usual guarantees of authenticity and related issues as if buying from a live sale. You wouldn't be able to view the item unless, of course, the item was put on the site by one of the specialist associated dealers and you arranged to view the piece or pieces with the dealer during the period it was on the site. Yes, it is possible to view pieces in this way but of course the dealer will of course not be allowed to have the piece or pieces for sale anywhere else or in any other manner whilst they are on the site. You can also ask a dealer for further images or more detailed images to enable you to get a better picture of the piece.

What does the future hold? 360 degree video images of objects? There are already such images available on the sothebys.com online site but usually reserved for 'special' or 'promotional' items.

Paper, printing, postage, costs, etc, etc are all becoming more and more expensive. In years to come, on-line sales for the low to middle value of antiques and collectables may be the only viable alternative.

Some Examples of Auction Prices

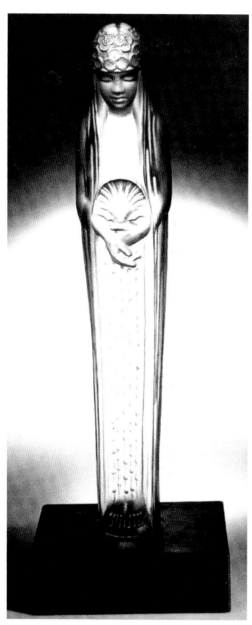

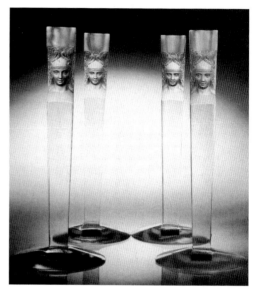

*Two pairs of **Caritide** frosted glass candlesticks, with sepia staining, 28cm high (lacking detachable sconces, some damage) £12,375/$21,040. (Christie's South Ken)*

A tall Galatee frosted glass figure, on a wooden base, 56.5cm high (with minor chips) £7875/$13,387. (Christie's South Ken)

*A **Deux Sirenes** circular box and cover, 26cm diameter £2025/$3445. (Christie's South Ken)*

*A clear and frosted **Jaffa** lemonade set (eight pieces). £731/$1250. (Christie's South Ken)*

*A frosted glass **Feuilles de Murier** table lamp, 36cm high (minor damage). £3150/$5355. (Christie's South Ken)*

*A **Muguet** frosted glass clock, 21.5cm high. £3600/$6120. (Christie's South Ken)*

Above: A set of 12 **Colmar** *wine glasses, 23cm high. £843/$1430. (Christie's South Ken)*

An electric blue **Escargot** *vase, 21.3cm high (plastic repair to foot and some ground out damage). £1237/$2100. (Christie's South Ken)*

A clear and frosted glass oval **Grande Ovale Joueuse de Flute** *ornament, 36.5cm high. £5625/ $9560. (Christie's South Ken)*

*A cased green glass **Poissons** vase, 23.5cm high £8000/$13600. (Bonhams)*

*A frosted opalescent and blue stained **Bacchantes** vase, 24.3cm high (foot reduced). £5500/$9350. (Bonhams)*

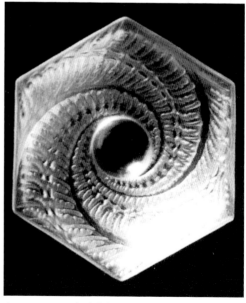

*A **Zinnias** frosted and blue stained box and cover, 10.1cm long. £400/$680. (Bonhams)*

*An aqua-green stained **Saint-Nectaire** box and cover, 8.5cm diameter. £300/$510. (Bonhams)*

A spherical cased opalescent **Druide** vase, 18cm high. £843/$1433. (Christie's South Ken)

An emerald green frosted glass **Languedoc** ovoid vase, 22.5cm high. £15187/$25820. (Christie's South Ken)

Left: Clear and frosted decoration of two budgerigars £2475/$4330. Right: **Feuilles de Vigne** clear and frosted ice bucket, 23cm high. £1000/$1700. Rear: **Ormeaux** dark amber oviform vase 17cm high. £960/$1680.

Front: **Ferrières** emerald green vase with everted rim. 17cm high. £1125/$1970. Rear: **Espalion** cased opalescent jade green vase, 18cm high. £2500/$4375.

Pan *Cristal Lalique frosted and silvered metal mounted table lamp. Made after 1951 it has fitments for electric use. 33cm high. £2800/$4900 (Bonhams).*

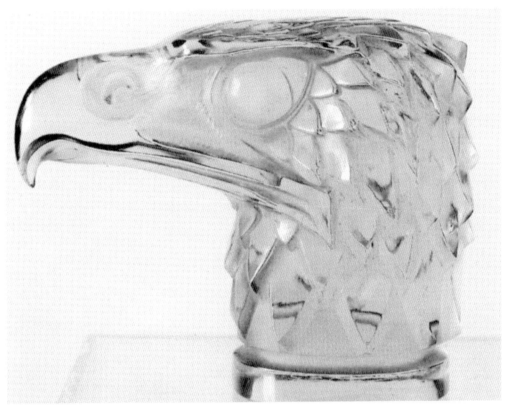

Tête d'Aigle clear and frosted amethyst-tinted car mascot. 10.7cm high. £2000/$3500.

Naïde clear and frosted glass ashtray, the circular bowl is surmounted by arched flat panel moulded with a mermaid. 10cm diam. £215/$372. **Lapin** opalescent glass ashtray, the circular dish surmounted in the centre by a rabbil. 10cm diam. £300/$525. **Gâtinais** clear and frosted preserve pot and cover moulded in the form of a flowerhead. 19.5cm diam. £450/$7875. **Amour** frosted galss book end in the form of a seated **Angel**. 18.5cm high. £250/$440.

*Design for a **Pegagus** twin handled shallow bowl of cameo shape drawn in pencil coloured with a blue/green body. The image area is 35 x 57.5cm and is unsigned. £800/$1400 (Bonhams)*

Tourbillons *frosted amber vase, 20.3cm high, £10000/$18500.*

Sirenes *opalescent frosted and blue-stained bowl. 35.6 diam. £3200/$5600.*

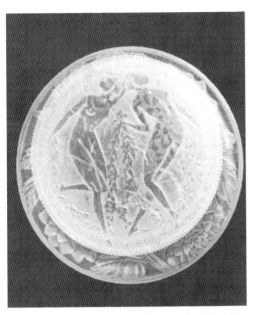

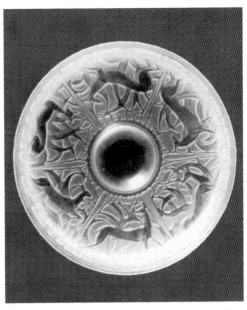

Poudre de Riz clear and frosted powder box with card base. 7cm diam. £600/$1050.

Chantilly clear and frosted box and cover. 8.6cm diam. £140/$245.

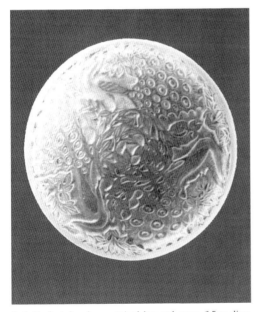

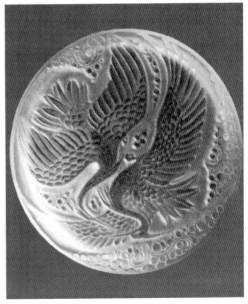

Isabelle frosted and grey-stained box and cover. 8.5cm diam. £600/$1050.

Rambouillet clear and frosted and sepia-stained box and cover, 8.5cm diam. £200/$370.

Faune frosted Brule Parfums. 21cm high. £100/$1/5.

Bibliography

Catalogue des Verreries de René Lalique – The Complete Illustrated Guide for 1932 reprinted by Dover Publications, New York, 1982.
Lalique Glass Nicholas M. Dawes, Viking, 1986.
Lalique – Jewellery and Glassware Tony L. Mortimer, Pyramid Books, 1989.
The Glass of Lalique – A Collector's Guide Christopher Vane Percy, Studio Vista, 1977.
Lalique Catalogue Raisonné, 1880–1945 Felix Marcilhac, 1989.
Jewellery of René Lalique Vivienne Becker, Goldsmith's Co. Exhibition, 1987. Published by Goldsmith's Co.
Perfume Bottles of Lalique Mary Lou and Glenn Utt, with Patricia Bayer, Crown Publishers, 1985.
The Art of René Lalique Patricia Bayer and Mark Waller, Quintet Publications Ltd, 1988.

General Glass Books

Glass – Art Nouveau to Art Deco Victor Arwas, Academy Editions, London.
Modern Fine Glass Leloise Davis Skelley, Garden City Publishing, New York, 1942.
Modern Glass Ada Polak, Faber & Faber, 1962.
Twentieth Century Design – Glass Frederick Cooke, Bell & Hyman, 1986.
Glass W. B. Honey, The Victoria & Albert Museum, published under the authority of the Ministry of Education, 1946.
Glass, A Guide for Collectors Gabriella Gross-Galliner, Frederick Muller Ltd 1970.
British Glass Between the Wars edited by Roger Dodsworth, A. H. Jolly Ltd for the Broadfield House Glass Museum.
Modern Glass Guillaume Janneau, The Studio Ltd, 1931.

Journals and Catalogues

The Studio – various issues
Lalique Car Mascots Breves Galleries, London (late 1920s)
Connoisseur 1920/30
Pottery & Glass Trades Review
Bonhams' Lalique catalogues
Christie's Lalique catalogues
Sotheby's Decorative Art catalogues

Further Information

If you want to keep up to date with what is going on in the contemporary Lalique scene then you can join the Lalique Society of America. This society publishes a quarterly magazine, in which as well as all the current promotion of new material, there are various articles on the works of Lalique, interviews with collectors and auction room up-dates.

For further details contact:

Lalique North America, Inc.
400 Veterans' Boulevard
Carlstadt, New Jersey NJ 07072
1-800-CRISTAL (274-7825) - (in US only)
e-mail: info@lalique.com

Information on the value, authenticity and identification of old or discontinued Lalique, including jewellery, may be obtained by sending phtotographs or details to:

Nicholas M. Dawes
Lalique Specialist
67 East 11th Street
New York. NY10003
Phone (212) 473 5111 Fax (212) 353 3845
email nmdawes@aol.com

Please include your telephone number. All information from Mr. Dawes is free of charge, with the exception of formal written appraisals.

You can also see exhibitions of René Lalique's glass held in the contemporary Lalique showrooms in London. Whilst these showrooms are specifically for the promotion of current Lalique, there are exhibitions of René's work from time to time.

For further information contact:
Showroom Manager
162 New Bond Street
London W1Y 9PA

collect2invest

a site full of information for the collector, in an ever changing world of collecta

 kids 2 collect

from pokemon to paddington bear,
a site for the younger collector

 appraisal & identification

submit your item on-line for our
team of experts to identify it, or
provide you with a full appraisal

 events

important auctions, both in
London & the provinces,
antique fairs for your diary, a
calendar of collecting.

 restoration

whatever the problem, we can
put you in touch with professional
restorers in your region

 book shop

specialist publications,
reference books & price
guides available to buy on-line

 on-line shopping

a selection of collectables and
antiques to buy on-line. buy
with confidence in a shop built
for collectors; genuine articles
verified by our team of experts

 investment members

an entrance to the advantages
of membership. non-members
can read all about the exclusive
benefits of membership,
existing members have
immediate access.

 contact us

contact our team

www.collect2invest.com